Student Solutions Manual to Accompany *Modern Macroeconomics*

Student Solutions Manual to Accompany *Modern Macroeconomics*

Sanjay K. Chugh

The MIT Press

Cambridge, Massachusetts

London, England

MIT Press books may be purchased at special quantity discounts for business or sales promotional use. For information, please email special_sales@mitpress.mit.edu or write to the Special Sales Department, The MIT Press, One Rogers Street, Cambridge, MA 02142.

ISBN: 978-0-262-52806-1

10 9 8 7 6 5 4 3 2 1

Contents

Chapter 1 Problem Set Solutions   1

Chapter 2 Problem Set Solutions   8

Chapter 3 Problem Set Solutions   19

Chapter 4 Problem Set Solutions   24

Chapter 5 Problem Set Solutions   29

Chapter 6 Problem Set Solutions   34

Chapter 7 Problem Set Solutions   36

Chapter 8 Problem Set Solutions   40

Chapter 9 Problem Set Solutions   47

Chapter 15 Problem Set Solutions   55

Chapter 16 Problem Set Questions   61

Chapter 17 Problem Set Solutions   89

Chapter 18 Problem Set Solutions   92

Chapter 19 Problem Set Solutions   93

Chapter 21 Problem Set Solutions   95

Chapter 22 Problem Set Solutions   104

Chapter 24 Problem Set Solutions   108

Chapter 25 Problem Set Solutions   113

Chapter 27 Problem Set Solutions   114

Chapter 28 Problem Set Solutions   123

Chapter 29 Problem Set Solutions   125

Chapter 30 Problem Set Questions   133

Chapter 31 Problem Set Solutions   141

Chapter 1 Problem Set Solutions

1. Sales Tax

a. The sales tax on good 1 is paid in addition to its price P_1. Thus the total expenditure on good 1 (i.e., the total amount of money the consumer will pay out of his pocket to purchase good 1) is $(1+t_1)P_1c_1$. For example, in Massachusetts the sales tax rate is 5 percent, so we would have $t_1 = 0.05$. This means that you would pay 105 percent $(1+t_1 = 1.05)$ of the before-tax price. Because there is no tax on good 2, the budget constraint is $(1+t_1)P_1c_1 + P_2c_2 = Y$.

b. If we solve the budget constraint for c_2 in terms of c_1, we get

$$c_2 = -\frac{P_1(1+t_1)}{P_2}c_1 + \frac{Y}{P_2}$$

and clearly the slope of the budget line is affected. This is an important general lesson: the reason why taxes levied on consumers have (or do not have) effects is because in general they alter the budget constraint. Intuitively, if the consumer now spent all of his income on good 1, he would be able to buy less than without the sales tax, but if spent all of his income on good 2, the quantity of good 2 he could buy would be unaffected by the imposition of the sales tax on good 1. Graphically, the budget line becomes steeper by pivoting around the vertical intercept, as shown in the figure below. Because the consumer's optimal choice of (c_1, c_2) is described by the tangency of an indifference curve with the budget line, the figure also shows how the optimal choice changes—in this case, the optimal choice moves from point A to point B. As drawn in the figure, the new optimal choice features less consumption of good 1 and more consumption of good 2—the consumer has substituted some good 2 for some good 1 in the face of a rise in price (inclusive of tax) of good 1. But see part c below for more on this substitution effect.

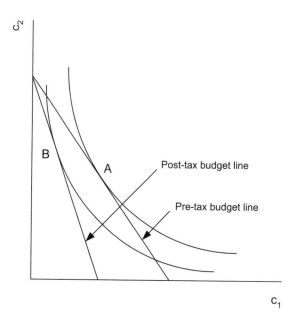

After the imposition of the sales tax on good 1, the optimal choice moves from point A to point B, which features less consumption of good 1.

c. The consumer's problem is to maximize $\ln c_1 + \ln c_2$ subject to the budget constraint $Y - P_1 c_1 - P_2 c_2 = 0$. The Lagrangian for this problem is

$$L(c_1, c_2, \lambda) = \ln c_1 + \ln c_2 + \lambda(Y - (1+t_1)P_1 c_1 - P_2 c_2),$$

where λ denotes the Lagrange multiplier on the budget constraint. The first-order conditions of L with respect to c_1, c_2, and λ are, respectively,

$$\frac{1}{c_1} - \lambda(1+t_1)P_1 = 0$$

$$\frac{1}{c_2} - \lambda P_2 = 0$$

$$Y - (1+t_1)P_1c_1 - P_2c_2 = 0$$

We must solve this system of equations for c_1 and c_2. There are, of course, many ways to solve this system, which only differ in the exact order of equations used. One useful way of proceeding is to first eliminate the multiplier λ. To do this, from the second equation, we get $\lambda = \frac{1}{P_2c_2}$. Substituting this into the first equation gives

$$\frac{1}{c_1} - \frac{P_1(1+t_1)}{P_2c_2} = 0.$$

From here, we can solve for P_2c_2, which is simply total expenditure on good 2:

$$P_2c_2 = (1+t_1)P_1c_1.$$

This expression states that total expenditure on good 2 equals total expenditure on good 1 (inclusive of the tax on good 1). Note that this result does not need always to hold; it holds here because of the given utility function.

Proceeding, substitute the expression above into the budget constraint to get

$$Y - (1+t_1)P_1c_1 - (1+t_1)P_1c_1 = 0,$$

from which it easily follows that the optimal choice of consumption of good 1 is

$$c_1^* = \frac{Y}{2(1+t_1)P_1}.$$

If we had numerical values for the objects on the right-hand side, clearly we would know numerically the optimal choice of consumption of good 1. This solution reveals that a rise in t_1 (holding constant Y and P_1) results in a fall in c_1^*.

To obtain the optimal choice of consumption of good 2, return to the above expression $P_2 c_2 = (1+t_1)P_1 c_1$, from which we get that consumption of good 2 is related to consumption of good 1 in the following way: $c_2 = \left(\dfrac{(1+t_1)P_1}{P_2} \right) c_1$. Inserting the optimal choice of good 1 found above, we have that the optimal choice of good 2 is

$$c_2^* = \frac{Y}{2P_2}.$$

Thus, even though the consumer splits his income evenly on expenditures on good 1 and good 2, consumption of good 1 and good 2 are not the same unless $t_1 = 0$. But notice from the expression above that the optimal choice of good 2 is independent of the tax rate on good 1! Thus, if we plot this utility function and the associated optimal choices as in part b above, we would get a movement of the optimal choice straight left from point A, the original optimal choice, meaning the optimal choice of good 2 is identical while the optimal choice of good 1 decreases.

3. **A Canonical Utility Function**

a. With $\sigma = 0$, the utility function becomes the linear function $u(c) = c - 1$, which has a simple graph:

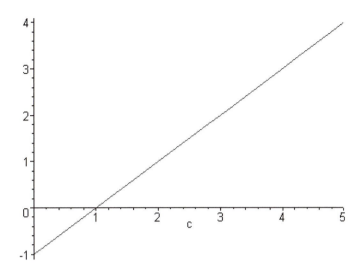

Notice that utility may actually be negative—but recall that the units of utility (utils) are completely arbitrary, so there is nothing wrong with considering negative values of utility. This linear function clearly does not display diminishing marginal utility because its slope is constant at one throughout—so, of course, marginal utility never becomes negative either.

b. With $\sigma = 1/2$, the utility function becomes $u(c) = 2\sqrt{c} - 2$, which looks like

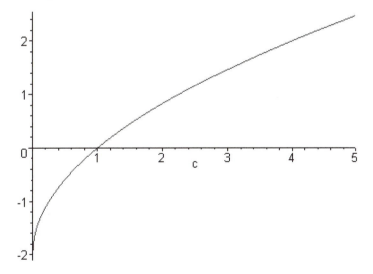

Notice again that here we have negative values of utility, which is fine since utility is measured in an arbitrary scale. The slope of this utility function is $u'(c) = 1/\sqrt{c}$ (recall the slope of a function is simply the first derivative), which is always positive as long as

consumption is positive, so marginal utility is never negative. And clearly as consumption

rises, the slope falls, so this function does display diminishing marginal utility.

c. The natural log utility function has graph

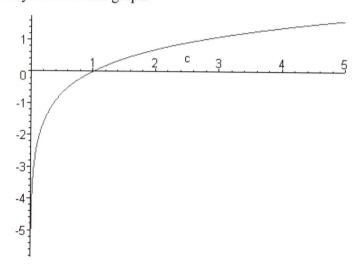

The derivative of this function is $u'(c) = 1/c$, which is always positive when

consumption is positive, so this function also does not ever experience negative marginal

utility. As consumption rises, the slope of the utility function falls, so this function does

display diminishing marginal utility.

d. The derivative of the log utility function is $u'(c) = 1/c$, while the derivative of the general

utility function presented above is $u'(c) = c^{-\sigma}$. Clearly, for $\sigma = 1$ the slopes of the two

functions (that is, the two marginal utility functions) are identical. This does not prove that

the two functions are identical, however, because it could be that the two functions always

have the same slope but are vertical translates of each other. To see that they are indeed the

same function, however, try plotting the general utility function for several values of the

curvature parameter near one (i.e., try plotting the function for, say,

$\sigma = 0.9, \sigma = 0.95, \sigma = 0.99, \sigma = 1.05, \sigma = 1.01$, etc.)—you will see that as the curvature parameter approaches one from either direction, the general utility function approaches the log utility function.

Chapter 2 Problem Set Solutions

1. Interaction of Consumption Tax and Wage Tax

a. The representative agent's net income from working is now given by $Y = (1-t_n) \cdot W \cdot n$,

where t_n is the labor tax rate and the other notation is the same as in chapter 2. He spends all

of this income on consumption, which now costs $P \cdot (1+t_c)$ dollars per unit (inclusive of the

consumption tax). Using the fact that $n = 1 - l$ in the weekly model, equating the

representative agent's labor income with his expenditures on consumption gives us

$$P \cdot (1+t_c) \cdot c = (1-t_n) \cdot W \cdot (1-l).$$

If we multiply out the right-hand side of this expression and then move the term

involving the labor tax rate to the left-hand side we obtain

$$P \cdot (1+t_c) \cdot c + (1-t_n) \cdot W \cdot l = (1-t_n) \cdot W.$$

Then, solving this last expression for c, we arrive at

$$c = \frac{(1-t_n) \cdot W}{(1+t_c) \cdot P} - \frac{(1-t_n) \cdot W}{(1+t_c) \cdot P} l.$$

This last expression can now readily be graphed with consumption on the vertical axis

and leisure on the horizontal axis. As in the standard model, the horizontal intercept is $l = 1$.

However, the slope is now

$$-\frac{(1-t_n) \cdot W}{(1+t_c) \cdot P}.$$

8

Clearly, if we set the consumption tax rate to zero, we recover the budget constraint in our standard consumption-leisure model—in fact the model we studied in chapter 2 is simply a special case of the model here. The reason the budget constraint differs here from the standard model is simple: the consumption tax is yet another tax for the consumer to take account of when making his choices about consumption and leisure. No matter the model under consideration, the budget constraint always describes all the relevant trade-offs between two alternative use of resources, and the relevant tradeoffs involve all taxes.

b. From the analysis in part a above, we see that the slope of the budget constraint depends on the relative tax $(1-t_n)/(1+t_c)$ (in addition to the term W/P, but you are told to assume that W and P remain constant). Under the current tax policy of a 20 percent wage tax and zero consumption tax, the relative tax is $(1-0.20)/(1+0) = 0.80$. So the slope of the representative agent's budget constraint is currently $-0.80W/P$, on which he makes some optimal choice of consumption and leisure.

Now the government wants to lower the labor tax rate to $t_n = 0.15$ but wants to leave the representative agent's optimal choice of consumption and leisure unchanged. This means that whatever the government does, it must make sure that the slope of his budget constraint does not change—which means that the relative tax must remain 0.80. We can then solve for the new consumption tax rate that yields this relative tax: $(1-0.15)/(1+t_c) = 0.80$ means that the government must set a consumption tax rate of $t_c = 0.0625$. The economic reasoning is that the relative tax has two free variables in it, the labor tax and the consumption tax. There are an infinite number of combinations that yield any particular value of the relative tax. Think of the following simple example: if you have two numbers x and y, and you are asked to come up with a combination of the two variables such that $x/y = 0.80$, there are obviously an infinite number of combinations that work.

c. The statement is true, and it follows from the discussion given in part b above. If the government believes that W and P are unaffected by its tax policies (which is not true—we will address this issue soon), then it has two tax rates it can alter to achieve its goals, but it is only the relative tax that affects the representative agent's budget constraint.

d. We saw in the standard consumption-leisure model that as the budget line became steeper, consumption increases. This is still true in this version of the consumption-leisure model. The current tax policy has $t_n = 0.20$ and $t_c = 0$ so that the relative tax is $(1-0.20)/(1+0) = 0.80$. Any new tax policy which features a larger value of $(1-t_n)/(1+t_c)$ (and hence a steeper budget constraint) will thus achieve the desired goal of higher overall consumption. With a labor tax rate of $t_n = 0.15$, we thus need

$$\frac{(1-0.15)}{(1+t_c)} > 0.80.$$

Solving this inequality for t_c, we have that

$$t_c < 0.0625$$

achieves the desired goal. So any tax policy with $t_n = 0.15$ and $t_c < 0.0625$ achieves the desired policy role. So the conclusion is: yes, the consumption tax rate can be raised and the desired goal still be achieved.

e. The Lagrangian is

$$L(c,l,\lambda) = u(c,l) + \lambda\left[(1-t_n)W(1-l) - P(1+t_c)c\right].$$

The FOCs with respect to consumption and leisure are (we'll ignore the one with respect to the multiplier because we actually don't need it to generate the consumption-leisure optimality condition):

$$u_c(c,l) - \lambda P(1+t_c) = 0$$
$$u_l(c,l) - \lambda W(1-t_n) = 0$$

To generate the consumption-leisure optimality condition, we must combine these two expressions by eliminating λ between them. Doing so, and expressing one side of the resulting expressing as the MRS between consumption and leisure, we have

$$\frac{u_l(c,l)}{u_c(c,l)} = \frac{(1-t_n)W}{(1+t_c)P}.$$

The left-hand side is the representative consumer's MRS between consumption and leisure, and the right-hand side is the real wage rate (W/P) adjusted by both the labor and consumption taxes.

3. A Backward-Bending Aggregate Labor Supply Curve?

a. In the table below, the aggregate (total) number of hours worked by all persons in the

economy at each wage rate is now shown (this was not given to you).

Nominal Wage, W	Person A	Person B	Person C	Person D	Person E	Aggregate
$10	20 hours	0 hours	0 hours	0 hours	0 hours	20 hours
$15	25	15	0	0	0	40
$20	30	22	8	0	0	60
$25	33	27	15	5	0	80
$30	35	30	20	15	0	100
$35	37	32	25	20	6	120
$40	36	31	27	25	21	140
$45	35	30	26	28	30	149
$50	33	29	24	25	29	140

The aggregate labor supply curve simply plots the values in the last column in the table

above against the wage rate (with, recall, the labor tax rate held constant at $t_n = 0$ throughout

for simplicity), as shown below. Clearly, most of the aggregate labor supply curve is upward-

sloping, with only the very top portion backward-bending. For brevity, the individuals' labor

supply curves are omitted—they are, of course, simply each individual's hours worked

plotted against the wage, and it should be clear even from the table that each individual in the

economy has a backward-bending labor supply curve.

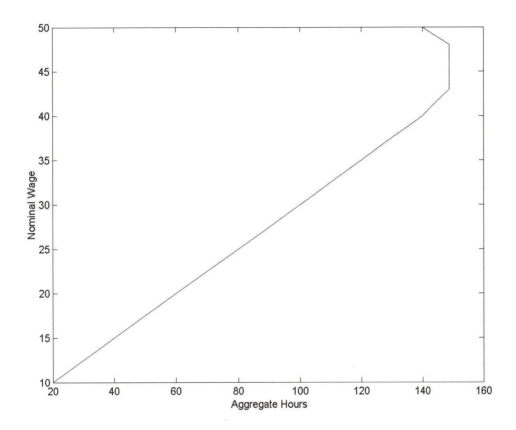

Now suppose that in this economy, the "usual" range of the nominal wage is between $10 and $45.

b. If the usual range of the nominal wage is $10–$45 in the economy, then clearly no (see the figure above), the aggregate labor supply is not backward-bending.

c. The point of the representative-agent framework is to represent theoretically the "average" person in the economy in all aspects of his economic life (in so far as such theoretical modeling is possible…), including of course his labor supply decisions. The "average" person in the economy does not earn the highest wages in the economy.

d. Over the range $10–$45, the labor supply curves of person A, person B, and person C are backward-bending, while the labor supply curves of person D and person E are not (notice that the labor supply curves of person D and person E do not bend backwards until the range

$45–$50). The aggregate labor supply curve is always upward-sloping in this range of the wage. The fundamental issue here is that people are different from each other in such a way that the average person, over the range $10–$45, "looks like" only 2 of the 5 people in this economy (person D and person E). We could easily construct another example in which the representative agent's labor supply "looked like" well less than 40% of the population over some "usual" range of income. This illustrates that microeconomic phenomena (in this case the backward-bending labor supply curve) when summed together do not necessarily give qualitatively the same phenomena at the macroeconomic level—a cautionary note in using the representative-agent approach to macroeconomics.

5. European and US Consumption-Leisure Choices

a. If Europeans work fewer hours than Americans, then Europeans have more leisure time than Americans, simply because (in our weekly framework) $n + l = 168$. Europeans and Americans have identical utility functions, which means that their indifference maps are identical. This means that the difference in hours worked must arise completely from differences in their budget constraints. With a higher labor income tax in Europe, the budget constraint of the European consumer is less steep than the budget constraint of the American, as the diagram below shows (because the slope of the budget constraint is $(1-t)W/P$, and you are given that W/P is the same in the two countries). The diagram shows that the European optimally chooses more leisure (hence less labor) and less consumption than the American. Here the difference between Europeans and Americans is solely in the relative prices (embodied by the slope of the budget constraint) they face. (For full credit here, you had to somehow make clear that the indifference maps of the representative European and the representative American are identical.)

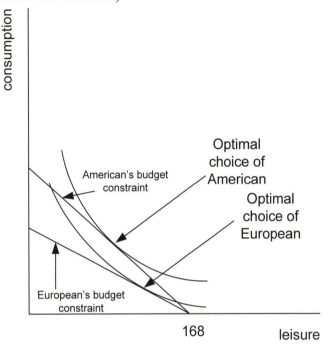

b. In this case the budget constraints of the European consumer and American consumer are identical, so the difference in hours worked must arise completely from differences in their utility functions. Graphically, this means that the two types of consumers have different indifference maps (i.e., a different set of indifference curves). In the diagram below, the budget line is the common budget line of the European and the American. The solid indifference curves are the American's, while the dashed indifference curves are the European's. With steeper indifference curves, the European's optimal choice along the same budget line must occur at a point that features more leisure (hence less labor) and less consumption than the American's optimal choice. Here, the difference between Europeans and Americans is solely in their preferences.

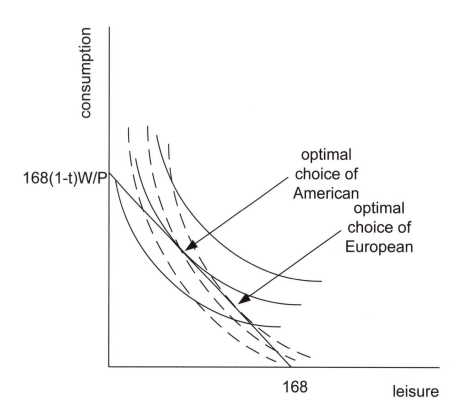

consumption

168(1-t)W/P

optimal
choice of
American

optimal
choice of
European

168   leisure

7. Quasi-linear Utility

a. Marginal utility with respect to consumption is the slope of the utility function when viewed as a function of consumption alone. The given function is logarithmic in consumption, and the natural log function, is strictly increasing and strictly concave, meaning the slope with respect to consumption is always decreasing and asymptotes to zero. Hence this function does display diminishing marginal utility in consumption.

b. Just as above, marginal utility with respect to leisure is the slope of the utility function when viewed as a function of leisure alone. The given function is linear in leisure, hence its slope with respect to leisure is constant. Thus this function does not display diminishing marginal utility in leisure.

c. (NOTE: If you can solve this problem without setting up a Lagrangian, you may do so.) The consumption-leisure optimality condition (which can be derived using a Lagrangian, which is omitted here because the general derivation proceeds exactly as we've seen several times) is

$$\frac{u_l}{u_c} = \frac{A}{1/c} = (1-t) \cdot w,$$

from which we get that $Ac = (1-t)w$ at the consumer's optimal choice. Substituting the given budget constraint into this (i.e., substituting for c) we have $A \cdot (1-t) \cdot w \cdot n = (1-t) \cdot w$. Canceling terms and solving for n, we find

$$n = \frac{1}{A},$$

which shows that labor supply here is independent of taxes, hence changes in the tax rate cannot affect the quantity of labor. The labor supply function, plotted with the wage (before- or after-tax, it doesn't make a difference) on the vertical axis and n on the horizontal axis, is a vertical line at the numerical value $1/A$.

Further discussion: The reason why labor (equivalently, leisure) here doesn't depend at all on the (before- or after-tax) wage is that there is no diminishing marginal utility in leisure (i.e., utility is linear with respect to leisure, as we saw above). When a multi-dimensional utility function is linear in one argument and has diminishing marginal utility in its other argument(s), it is said to be "quasi-linear." Quasi-linear utility functions give rise to demand functions for the linear object that are completely insensitive (inelastic) to price—here, the demand for leisure (the flip side of which is the supply of labor) is completely insensitive (inelastic) to the wage.

Chapter 3 Problem Set Solutions

1. The Wealth Effect on Consumption

a. Recall from the standard two-period consumption-savings model that when plotting the lifetime budget constraint (LBC) with c_2 on the vertical axis and c_1 on the horizontal axis, the price P_1 affects the slope but not the vertical intercept. It follows that if P_1 rises, then the vertical intercept is unaffected but the budget line becomes steeper. As shown in the figure below, this can lead to lower consumption in period 1.

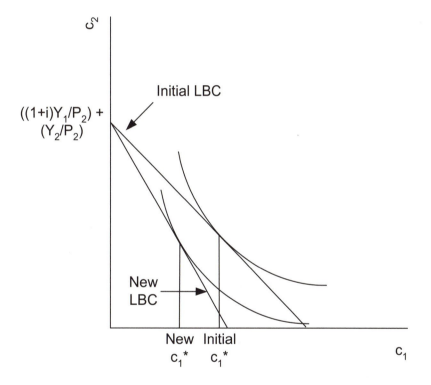

Notice that as drawn, the optimal choice of c_2 has also fallen. There is nothing in the structure of the model as we have discussed it that can lead us to definitively conclude that this must be the case—however, it is the most likely case.

b. We saw that the LBC in the two-period model is

$$P_1 c_c + \frac{P_2 c_2}{(1+i)} = Y_1 + \frac{Y_2}{(1+i)} + (1+i)A_0 \,.$$

19

If we keep $A_0 \neq 0$, then solving for c_2 gives us the LBC

$$c_2 = -\left(\frac{P_1(1+i)}{P_2}\right)c_1 + \left(\frac{1+i}{P_2}\right)Y_1 + \frac{Y_2}{P_2} + \left(\frac{(1+i)^2}{P_2}\right)A_0.$$

Clearly, A_0 (regardless of whether it is positive or negative) affects only the intercepts of the LBC but not the slope. Thus a decrease in A_0 leads to a parallel shift inwards of the LBC, thus leading to a fall in the optimal choice of c_1 as shown in the figure below.

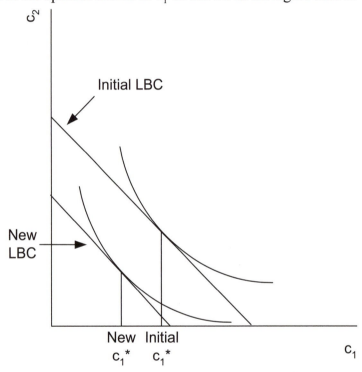

c. The perfectly rational representative-agent considers all his lifetime resources (both labor income as well as initial wealth) when making his optimal consumption-savings decision. Thus, both the change in price in part a and the change in initial wealth in part b (as well as possible changes in the nominal interest rate, the price of consumption in period 2, or labor income in either period!) have their effect by impacting the real value (as opposed to nominal value) of lifetime resources. The real value of lifetime resources is sometimes called "lifetime wealth"—thus it is lifetime wealth that the individual considers when making his optimal consumption-savings choice.

3. Mechanics of the Consumption-Savings Model

a. A rise in the price level in period 1 lowers real labor income in period 1 because $y_1 = Y_1 / P_1$ and Y_1 remains constant by assumption. Real labor income in period 2 is unaffected. The LBC becomes steeper because, recall, the slope of the LBC is $-(P_1(1+i)/P_2)$. The vertical intercept is unaffected because P_1 does not enter the expression for the vertical intercept of the LBC in nominal terms. These effects are shown in the figure below:

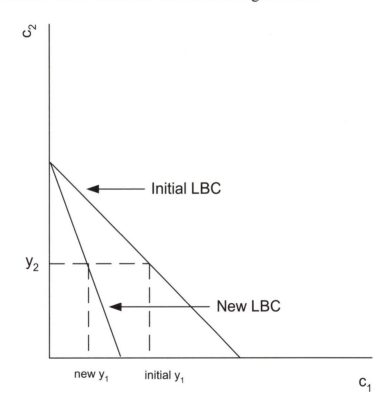

b. A rise in the price level in period 2 lowers real labor income in period 2 because $y_2 = Y_2 / P_2$ and Y_2 remains constant by assumption. Real labor income in period 1 is unaffected. The LBC becomes flatter because, recall again, the slope of the LBC is $-(P_1(1+i)/P_2)$. Here the vertical intercept is now lower because P_2 does enter the expression for the vertical intercept of the LBC in nominal terms, and it is the horizontal intercept that remains fixed. These effects are shown in the figure below:

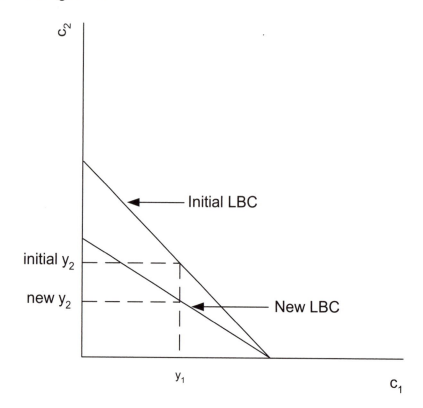

(NOTE: In both questions 1a and 1b, you might have been thrown off if you were trying to use the analogous diagram in the chapter, in which you see that both y_1 and y_2 affect the vertical intercept. If you tried to base your analysis on this diagram and your answers were incorrect, it is probably because you failed to take account of the fact that the real interest rate rises in an exactly offsetting way in part a and falls in an exactly offsetting way in part b.) This points out that the LBC in nominal terms and the LBC in real terms highlight different issues. In any given problem it is usually more straightforward to use one rather than the other. As you might expect, when you are considering changes in nominal variables (prices, nominal interest rate, inflation), it is usually more straightforward to use the LBC in nominal terms.

c. Real labor income in both periods is unaffected by the change in the nominal interest rate. The rise in i makes the LBC steeper by pivoting around the unchanged point (y_1, y_2), as shown in the diagram below:

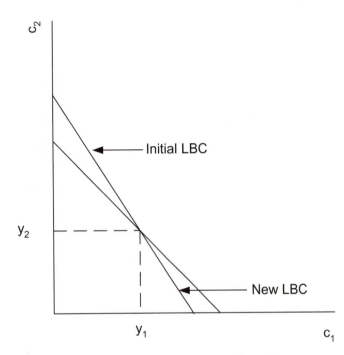

Chapter 4 Problem Set Solutions

1. **Optimal Choice in the Consumption-Savings Model with Credit Constraints: A Numerical Analysis**

a. The consumer's problem is to maximize lifetime utility—given by $u(c_1, c_2)$ subject to the LBC. The Lagrangian for this problem is thus

$$L(c_1, c_2, \lambda) = u(c_1, c_2) + \lambda \left(a_0 + y_1 + \frac{y_2}{1+r_1} - c_1 - \frac{c_2}{1+r_1} \right),$$

where we must include the nonzero initial real wealth a_0. The first-order conditions with respect to c_1 and c_2 are

$$u_1(c_1, c_2) - \lambda = 0$$
$$u_2(c_1, c_2) - \frac{\lambda}{1+r_1} = 0$$

Combining these, we get the usual consumption-savings optimality condition, $u_1(c_1, c_2) = (1 + r_1)u_2(c_1, c_2)$ (i.e., the MRS equals the slope of the LBC). Using the given utility function, at the optimal choice the following condition must be satisfied:

$$\frac{1}{2\sqrt{c_1}} = (1 + r_1)\frac{\beta}{2\sqrt{c_2}}.$$

Solving this expression for c_2 as a function of c_1 gives $c_2 = (1 + r_1)^2 \beta^2 c_1$. With the specific values given, this turns out to be $c_2 = c_1$. Substituting this into the lifetime budget constraint then yields

24

$$c_1 + \frac{c_1}{1+r_1} = a_0 + y_1 + \frac{y_2}{1+r_1}.$$

Solving for c_1 gives

$$c_1 = \left[\frac{1+r_1}{2+r_1}\right]\left[a_0 + y_1 + \frac{y_2}{1+r_1}\right],$$

which, when using the values provided, yields $c_1 = 7.90$ and hence $c_2 = 7.90$. Note that although you were not asked to compute it, you could find the implied value for a_1 using the period-1 budget constraint $c_1 + a_1 = a_0 + y_1$. This yields that $a_1 = -1.9$, indicating that the household chooses to be a debtor at the end of period 1.

b. The imposition of these credit constraints will be binding on the consumer's behavior. That is, it will alter the choices made by the household, as can be seen from the fact that in the absence of the credit constraints in part a, the consumer chose to be in debt at the end of period 1. Now, being restricted to hold a nonnegative asset position at the end of period 1, it will choose that asset position closest to its unrestricted choice but which also satisfies the credit constraint—that is, the consumer will choose $a_1 = 0$. The period-1 budget constraint, $c_1 + a_1 = a_0 + y_1$ then implies that $c_1 = 6$. The household will simply consume all it can in period 1, which is the sum of its endowment and initial assets (inclusive of interest income on those initial assets). It remains now to solve for c_2. Examining the period-2 budget constraint, $c_2 + a_2 = (1+r_1)a_1 + y_2$ with the condition $a_2 = 0$ imposed and $B_1^* = 0$ shows that $c_2 = y_2 = 10$. Extension: At this credit-constrained choice of consumption, the MRS clearly does not equal the slope of the LBC. The slope of the LBC is the market interest rate $1 + r$, as usual. However, we can define an "effective interest rate" for this consumer, which is the interest rate that would need to prevail for the choice $c_1 = 6, c_2 = 10$ to be the unrestricted optimal choice. We can obtain this from the condition $u_1(c_1,c_2) = (1+r)u_2(c_1,c_2)$. This condition is the same as where we started question 1a with, except now, knowing values for c_1 and c_2, we will use it to determine the consumer's effective interest rate. Plugging the values $c_1 = 6, c_2 = 10$ into this condition and solving for the interest rate gives us $r = 0.42$ as the effective interest rate, the interest rate that would have made this choice the consumer's unrestricted optimal choice.

c. With the values for consumption in each of the two periods from parts a and b, the utility function shows that utility without credit constraints equals $u(c_1,c_2) = 5.34$ and utility with credit constraints is $u(c_1,c_2) = 5.29$. Utility is lower under credit constraints, thus welfare is reduced by their imposition. This should strike you as sensible—the consumer wanted (rationally and with perfect information) to be in debt at the end of period 1, but banks were unwilling to lend, thus the consumer is worse off. Graphically, this means that the chosen consumption bundle under credit constraints lies on an indifference curve lower than the chosen consumption bundle in the absence of credit constraints. (TECHNICAL NOTE: You cannot say something like, "welfare is not lowered by much" because of credit constraints. Although we did not discuss it, the numbers attached to the utility function themselves have no economic meaning—all they are used for is comparing relative welfare, not for making any absolute statements about welfare. You are not responsible for knowing this technical detail, but this is useful to know.)

d. Using exactly the same solution procedure as in part a, we get that $c_1 = 10$ and $c_2 = 10$. Implied by this choice of consumption is that $a_1 = 0$ (due to the period-1 budget constraint).

That is, the optimal choice of the consumer following the positive income shock involves a zero asset position at the end of period 1.

e. With the credit constraint now back in place (with $y_1 = 9$), there will be no change in household behavior relative to the case without the credit constraint. That is, in part d, the optimal choice of households already involves a choice for a_1 that satisfies the credit constraint. Thus the credit constraint is not binding, and welfare is unaffected.

3. Two-Period Economy in Nominal Units

a. The inflation rate is easily computed as $\pi_2 = \dfrac{P_2}{P_1} - 1 = \dfrac{105}{100} - 1 = 0.05$. Then, using the exact Fisher equation, write $1 + r = \dfrac{1+i}{1+\pi_2} = \dfrac{1.05}{1.05} = 1$, so that $r = 0$.

b. The inflation rate is easily computed as $\pi_2 = \dfrac{P_2}{P_1} - 1 = \dfrac{105}{100} - 1 = 0.05$. Then, using the exact Fisher equation, write $1 + r = \dfrac{1+i}{1+\pi_2} = \dfrac{1.05}{1.05} = 1$, so that $r = 0$.

c. The familiar consumption-savings optimality condition is $\dfrac{u_1(c_1, c_2)}{u_2(c_1, c_2)} = 1 + r$. As we just saw above, for the given utility function, this becomes $\dfrac{1/c_1}{1} = 1 + r$, or after rearranging,

$$c_1 = \frac{1}{1+r}.$$

For the consumption-savings optimality condition associated with this particular utility function (which is quasi-linear in period-2 consumption), r seems to affect only the period-1 optimal choice of consumption and does not affect the growth rate of consumption across periods. Since you were asked to base your analysis on the consumption-savings optimality condition, the conclusion would thus be that r is not at all related to the rate of consumption growth for this utility function, instead affecting only the short-run level of consumption.

However, it is the case that in the full solution to the problem (i.e., using the consumption-savings optimality condition in tandem with the consumer's lifetime budget constraint to solve jointly for both short-run and long-run consumption), c_2 rises when r rises (to see this, substitute the consumption-savings optimality condition into the LBC, and solve for c_2). The fact that c_2 rises when r rises coupled with the result that c_1 falls when r rises means that indeed the consumption growth rate between period 1 and period 2 rises when r rises. You were not required to take the analysis this far since you were asked only to base the analysis on the consumption-savings optimality condition—but if you decided to take this route you had to use it correctly.

Many answers also simply discussed vaguely the consumption-savings optimality condition to argue something—you were told to base the analysis on the given utility function, so a general analysis did not address the issue.

Finally, note that simply arguing/explaining here that a rise in the real interest rate leads to a fall in period-1 consumption does not address the question—the question is about the rate of change of consumption between period 1 and period 2, not about the level of consumption in period 1 by itself.

Chapter 5 Problem Set Solutions

1. Intertemporal Consumption-Labor Model—Numerical Look 1

Note that you needed to compute the marginal utility functions. For the given lifetime utility function, the marginal utility functions are, for $t = 1,2$:

$$v_{c_t} = \frac{\sqrt{B_t}}{\sqrt{c_t}}; \; v_{l_t} = \frac{1}{\sqrt{l_t}}.$$

a. As by now is routine, the consumption-leisure marginal rate of substitution function is $MRS_{c_t l_t} = v_{l_t} / v_{c_t}$. With the given functions, the marginal rate of substitution function in period t, where t is either 1 or 2, is thus

$$MRS_{c_t l_t}(c_t, l_t) = \frac{\sqrt{c_t}}{\sqrt{B_t}\sqrt{l_t}}.$$

   Again, note that this function is the MRS function for period $t = 1,2$. From this function it is clear that a rise in B_t lowers this MRS, meaning a rise in B_t flattens the indifference map over consumption and leisure within a given period.

b. Again as by now should be routine, the intertemporal MRS function is given by $MRS_{c_1 c_2} = v_{c_1} / v_{c_2}$. Note the subscripts: v_{c_1} denotes the marginal utility function with respect to period-1 consumption, and v_{c_2} denotes the marginal utility function with respect to period-2 consumption. Using the given v_c function, we have

$$MRS_{c_1 c_c}(c_1, c_2) = \frac{\sqrt{B_1}}{\sqrt{B_2}} \cdot \frac{\sqrt{c_2}}{\sqrt{c_1}}.$$

The ratio of B values across the two periods affects the slope of the indifference map between period-1 and period-2 consumption. The larger is the ratio B_1 / B_2, the steeper is the indifference map across consumption in the two periods—the interpretation of this is that the larger is B_1 relative to B_2, the more "confident" (recall the interpretation of B given in the chapter) consumers are about the present (period 1) than they are about the future (period 2), hence the more period-2 consumption they are willing to give up for a given increase in period-1 consumption (which is our usual interpretation of the slope of an indifference curve with c_1 plotted on the horizontal axis and c_2 plotted on the vertical axis).

c. The LBC in real terms is

$$c_1 + \frac{c_2}{1+r} = (1-t_1)w_1(1-l_1) + \frac{(1-t_2)w_2(1-l_2)}{1+r}. \tag{1}$$

This LBC involves the four unknowns, c_1, c_2, l_1, and l_2, which are the variables you are asked to solve for. We need three other expressions involving these variables—these three are the two consumption-leisure optimality conditions (one for each of period 1 and period 2) and the one consumption-savings optimality condition. By now you should know how these optimality conditions can be obtained by formulating the appropriate Lagrangian—for ease of exposition the Lagrangian is omitted here. Suffice it to say it is simply the above consumption-leisure and consumption-savings optimality conditions that emerge from the Lagrangian. The consumption-leisure optimality conditions for period 1 and period 2 and the consumption-savings optimality condition are, respectively,

$$MRS_{c_1 l_1} = \frac{\sqrt{c_1}}{\sqrt{B_1}\sqrt{l_1}} = (1-t_1)w_1, \tag{2}$$

$$MRS_{c_2 l_2} = \frac{\sqrt{c_2}}{\sqrt{B_2}\sqrt{l_2}} = (1 - t_2)w_2, \tag{3}$$

$$MRS_{c_1 c_2} = \frac{\sqrt{B_1}}{\sqrt{B_2}}\frac{\sqrt{c_2}}{\sqrt{c_1}} = 1 + r \tag{4}$$

By now you should know the interpretation of these optimality conditions: they simply represent the tangency between a relevant budget constraint and a relevant indifference curve. Equations (1), (2), (3), and (4) are now four equations in the four unknowns c_1, c_2, l_1, and l_2, so we can solve with some algebraic effort.

Let's decide to express the unknowns c_2, l_1, and l_2 all in terms of c_1. Once we have done this, we can substitute into the LBC and solve for c_1. From (4), we get that

$$c_2 = \frac{B_2}{B_1}(1 + r)^2 c_1; \tag{5}$$

from (2), we get that

$$l_1 = \left(\frac{1}{(1 - t_1)w_1}\right)^2 \frac{1}{B_1} c_1; \tag{6}$$

and from (3) we similarly get that

$$l_2 = \left(\frac{1}{(1 - t_2)w_2}\right)^2 \frac{1}{B_2} c_2. \tag{7}$$

In (7), we need to substitute out c_2 using (5) (because, recall, we are trying to express the unknowns in terms of c_1), giving us

$$l_2 = \left(\frac{1+r}{(1-t_2)w_2}\right)^2 \frac{1}{B_1} c_1 . \tag{8}$$

Now, substitute into the LBC using (5), (6), and (8). Doing so and collecting all the resulting terms involving c_1 on the left-hand side (you should perform these algebraic steps yourself) gives us

$$c_1 \cdot \left[1 + \frac{B_2}{B_1}(1+r) + \frac{1}{(1-t_1)w_1 B_1} + \frac{1+r}{(1-t_2)w_2 B_1}\right] = (1-t_1)w_1 + \frac{(1-t_2)w_2}{1+r}, \tag{9}$$

in which the only unknown, as desired, is c_1. Inserting all of the given numerical values, we finally find that $c_1^* = 0.0245$. Then, using (5), (6), and (8), we find that $c_2^* = 0.0390$, $l_1^* = 0.8493$, and $l_2^* = 0.8118$. The individual thus works $1 - 0.85 = 0.15$ hours per week in the first period and $1 - 0.8114 = 0.1886$ hours per week in the second period.

d. Recall that real private savings (inclusive of taxes is) income minus tax payments minus consumption. Given the solution above, total real income in period 1 is $(1-l_1)w_1 = 0.03$, of which the amount paid in taxes is $t_1(1-l_1)w_1 = 0.0045$. Disposable income (gross income less taxes) in period 1 is thus $0.03 - 0.0045 = 0.0255$. Subtracting period-1 consumption, we have that real savings in period 1 is $4.3052 - 4.1233 = 0.1819$. Because the consumer began period 1 with zero assets, at the end of period 1 his real asset position is thus 0.1819. (Then, with positive assets to begin period 2, the individual is able to consume more than his income in period 2—perform this calculation to verify this for yourself.)

e. Examining the solution (9), we see that B_2 enters the solution in only one place. It is easy to conclude from (9) that a higher value of B_2 will lead to a lower value of optimal period-1 consumption. Specifically, $c_1^* = 0.0238$, which then implies that $c_2^* = 0.0503$, $l_1^* = 0.8233$, and $l_2^* = 0.7857$.

With B_2 higher relative to B_1 (and with the particular way B enters the utility function, specifically, multiplying c), the consumer is more "confident" about the economic state in the future (period 2) than in the present (period 1). He thus works and consumes less in period 1, and works and consumes more in period 2 due to the rise in B_2. Savings in period 1 rises to $(1-t_2)w_2(1-l_2)-c_1 = 0.0191$, consistent with the increased desire to postpone consumption until period 2.

Chapter 6 Problem Set Solutions

1. Lags in Labor Hiring

With employees being contractually bound to ("owned by") firms, the period-t nominal profits of a firm are given by

$$PR_t = P_t f(k_t, n_t) + P_t k_t + P_t w_t n_t - P_t k_{t+1} - P_t w_t n_{t+1},$$

in which labor used in production in period t, n_t, is chosen in period $t-1$ (and thus labor used in production in period $t+1$, n_{t+1}, is chosen in period t. In analogy with our model with only capital predetermined, the employees of a firm are a valuable "asset," with total market value $P_t w_t n_t$. Notice that this term enters positively in period t profits, rather than negatively with non-predetermined labor. What enters negatively in period t profits here is the "purchase" of period $t+1$ labor, namely the term $-P_t w_t n_{t+1}$. In the two-period model, discounted nominal profits of the firm are therefore

$$PR = P_1 f(k_1, n_1) + P_1 k_1 + P_1 w_1 n_1 - P_1 k_2 - P_1 w_1 n_2 + \frac{P_2 f(k_2, n_2)}{1+i_i} + \frac{P_2 k_2}{1+i_i} + \frac{P_2 w_2 n_2}{1+i_i} - \frac{P_2 k_3}{1+i_i} - \frac{P_2 w_2 n_3}{1+i_i}$$

The usual zero-terminal assets condition in this case means that $k_3 = 0$ and $n_3 = 0$ (the latter, again, because labor should be thought of as an "asset" here). Focusing attention on the choice of n_2 (since n_1 was chosen in period $t-1$), the first-order condition of the lifetime profit function with respect to n_2 is

$$-P_1 w_1 + \frac{P_2 f_n(k_2, n_2)}{1+i_1} + \frac{P_2 w_2}{1+i_1} = 0.$$

This expression can be rearranged to yield (using the exact Fisher equation)

$$(1 + r_1)w_1 = f_n(k_2, n_2) + w_2 .$$

If the real wage were equal to one in each period, this condition would reduce to $r_1 = f_n(k_2, n_2)$, which would be almost identical to the condition we derived in chapter 6 regarding capital demand (except of course in that case f_k is the relevant marginal product rather than f_n). The expression $r_1 = f_n(k_2, n_2)$ shows that if firms must choose labor for period 2 in period 1, the real interest rate between period 1 and period 2 is a relevant price to consider—which makes sense because there is now an interest opportunity cost associated with hiring labor (i.e., "investment" in hiring).

In general, however, w_1 and w_2 are not one; hence the condition above is not exactly the same as the capital demand condition. In the capital demand condition, the real price of capital goods is the same as the real price of consumption (which is one)—note that in the chapter the discussion on capital goods and consumption goods assumes these to be the same goods (e.g., computers can be viewed as both consumption goods and capital goods), so the dollar price of each in our theoretical model is the same. The same is not true of labor—the nominal price of labor is W, which, in general, is different from P.

Chapter 7 Problem Set Solutions

1. Government and Credit Constraints in the Two-Period Economy

a. Using the government's LBC, find that $t_2 = 2.2$.

b. Using the same procedure as in question 1a above (specifically, starting with the condition that $u_1(c_1, c_2) = (1+r)u_2(c_1, c_2)$) and with the given functions, we get that at the optimal choice, $c_2 = (1+r)c_1$. Plugging this into the LBC of the economy and solving for c_1 yields $c_1 = \frac{1}{2}\left[y_1 - g_1 + \frac{y_2 - g_2}{1+r}\right]$, from which it immediately follows that $c_1 = 10$, which then implies that $c_2 = 11$.

c. With government purchases unchanged, a change in the timing of lump-sum taxes leads to no change in consumption and hence no change in national savings. This is the Ricardian Equivalence proposition—consumers increase their private savings after the tax cut in anticipation of the tax increase that must occur in period two.

d. Examine the period-1 budget constraint of the consumer: $c_1 + a_1 = y_1 - t_1$ (remember, the consumer has zero initial assets here). This expression, along with the value of $c_1 = 10$ you found in part b above, can be used to determine that $a_1 = -9$. Thus consumers optimally (i.e., under no credit constraints) want to be debtors at the end of period one. With the imposition of the credit constraints, consumers can no longer do so, and will choose $a_1 = 0$ because that is the closest they can get to their unrestricted choice while also satisfying the credit constraint. The period-1 budget constraint, with $a_1 = 0$, yields $c_1 = y_1 - t_1 = 1$. The credit constraint diminishes welfare because consumers are being forced to choose a consumption allocation different from the one they would otherwise choose—graphically, they are on a lower indifference curve than the one that maximizes utility subject to the LBC of the economy.

e. With $t_1 = 7$, the credit constraint is still binding, and $c_1 = y_1 - t_1 = 2$. Thus, because $s_1^{nat} = y_1 - c_1 - g_1$, national savings falls by exactly the amount by which consumption rises, which is one. This occurs because Ricardian equivalence fails if capital controls/borrowing constraints are binding (which is another reason, beyond distortionary taxes, why Ricardian equivalence fails). The reason here is that consumers were not at their unrestricted optimal choice to begin with—they wanted to consume more in period 1 than they were restricted to. Thus, any relaxation of their period-1 budget constraint (i.e., in the form of lower taxes in period 1) induces them to increase their consumption, dragging down national savings.

3. Government Debt Ceilings

a. Using the given numerical values and using the 2011 government budget constraint given above, it is straightforward to calculate $b_{2011} = -\$16$ trillion.

b. Using the given numerical values, the value for b_{2011} found in part a, and using the 2011 government budget constraint given above, it is straightforward to calculate $b_{2011} = -\$17$ trillion. Under federal law at the time, the US government's debt could not be larger than $16 trillion. This limit is known as the "debt ceiling."

c. No, the debt ceiling poses no problem for the fiscal policy plans for the year 2011. This is because the t and g plans call for a debt at the end of 2011 of $16 trillion, which does not exceed the ceiling.

d. Yes, the debt ceiling poses a problem for the fiscal policy plans for the year 2012. This is because the *t* and *g* plans call for a debt at the end of 2012 of $17 trillion, which violates the ceiling.

5. Government in the Two-Period Model

a. A lump-sum tax is one whose total incidence (i.e., total amount paid) depends in no way at all on any choices/decisions that an individual makes.

b. Because $r = 0$, the lifetime government budget constraint boils down to simply $g_1 + g_2 = t_1 + t_2$. Thus, before the policy proposal, the government is planning to (needs to) collect $t_1 + t_2 = 3 + 5 = 8$ total units (note that these are real goods, since everything here is specified in real terms) in taxes. Because government spending is not changing and $r = 0$, reducing period-1 tax collections by one unit necessarily means period-2 tax collection must rise by one unit— hence $t_2 = 6$ if the policy change is enacted.

c. The tax change will have no effect at all because Ricardian equivalence applies—the representative consumer will simply save the entire period-1 tax cut in anticipation of the tax hike which is coming in period 2.

For the rest of this problem, suppose that instead of living for two periods, each consumer only lives for one period in the two-period economy. Specifically, there is a set of consumers that comes into existence at the beginning of period 1, knowing that at the end of period 1 they will cease to exist. At the beginning of period 2, there is a completely different set of consumers that comes into existence, knowing that at the end of period 2 they (and the entire economy) will cease to exist. The consumers in period 2 have no relation to the consumers in period 1, and the consumers in period 1 do not care at all about the consumers in period 2.

The government, however, continues to exist for the entire two periods. Continue to suppose that taxes are lump-sum (and that there are no credit constraints).

d. As in part b, the government will still need to raise $t_2 = 6$ if the policy change is enacted.

e. However, because consumers in period 1 no longer have any "preference" for period-2 consumption (because they simply won't be around in period 2), period-1 consumers won't need to save the one-unit tax cut in period 1; hence period-1 consumption will rise by one unit.

Chapter 8 Problem Set Solutions

1. Infrequent Stock Transactions

In differentiating the lifetime Lagrangian, we now need to look forward two periods from period t in order to see the consequences (payoffs) of period-t asset holding decisions. Specifically, the terms in the Lagrangian (between period t and $t+2$ inclusive) that involve period-t choice variables (namely, c_t and a_t) are

$$
\begin{aligned}
&\left[u(c_t) + \lambda_t(S_t a_{t-2} + D_t a_{t-2} + Y_t - P_t c_t - S_t a_t)\right] + \\
&\left[\beta u(c_{t+1}) + \beta \lambda_{t+1}(S_{t+1} a_{t-1} + D_{t+1} a_{t-1} + Y_{t+1} - P_{t+1} c_{t+1} - S_{t+1} a_{t+1})\right] + \\
&\left[\beta^2 u(c_{t+2}) + \beta^2 \lambda_{t+2}(S_{t+2} a_t + D_{t+2} a_t + Y_{t+2} - P_{t+2} c_{t+2} - S_{t+2} a_{t+2})\right] + \dots
\end{aligned}
$$

Note carefully these terms. The ellipsis at the end indicate that the summation continues forever (since the consumer is assumed to maximize lifetime utility), but the terms written down are only ones that are important for the problem at hand: the consumer in period t chooses c_t and a_t and there are no other terms in the Lagrangian (i.e., there are no other budget constraints) that contain these quantities. Also note the as we move successive periods into the future, the discount factor β is exponentiated further.

The first-order condition with respect to c_t is

$$
u'(c_t) - \lambda_t P_t = 0,
$$

which is standard. Nonstandard is the first-order condition with respect to a_t:

$$
-\lambda_t S_t + \beta^2 \lambda_{t+2}(S_{t+2} + D_{t+2}) = 0.
$$

The two conditions above (including the analogous first-order condition with respect to consumption at time $t+2$) can be combined to give

$$\frac{u'(c_t)}{u'(c_{t+2})} = \beta^2 \left[\frac{S_{t+2} + D_{t+2}}{S_t} \cdot \frac{P_t}{P_{t+2}} \right],$$

which is analogous to the condition derived in the chapter with a one-period holding period for assets, except that the two-period holding period here means that period $t+2$ is the relevant future period in which to evaluate the marginal utility of consumption, stock price, dividend, and nominal price of consumption. Instead, we can solve for the period-t stock price,

$$S_t = \beta^2 \left[\frac{u'(c_{t+2})}{u'(c_t)} (S_{t+2} + D_{t+2}) \frac{P_t}{P_{t+2}} \right],$$

which indicates that it is period $t+2$ marginal utility, price level, stock price, and dividend that affects the stock price in period t. This should make sense because (by assumption) stock purchased in period t does not yield anything until period $t+2$, so the relevant decision horizon is a two-period horizon, which is reflected in the stock price in period t.

3. Habit Persistence in Consumption

a. Using the same notation developed in the chapter, the consumer's choice variables in period t are c_t and a_t. The relevant terms in the consumer's Lagrangian from period t onward are

$$\left[u(c_t, c_{t-1}) + \lambda_t (S_t a_{t-1} + D_t a_{t-1} + Y_t - P_t c_t - S_t a_t) \right] +$$
$$\left[\beta u(c_{t+1}, c_t) + \beta \lambda_{t+1} (S_{t+1} a_t + D_{t+1} a_t + Y_{t+1} - P_{t+1} c_{t+1} - S_{t+1} a_{t+1}) \right] + \dots$$

Notice carefully the terms here: utility in period t depends on consumption in t and $t-1$; hence utility in period $t+1$ depends on consumption in $t+1$ and t, and the timing on the asset's returns, reflecting the one-period holding period.

The first-order condition with respect to a_t is simply

$$-\lambda_t S_t + \beta \lambda_{t+1}(S_{t+1} + D_{t+1}) = 0,$$

which can be rearranged as usual to give $S_t = \beta\left[\dfrac{\lambda_{t+1}}{\lambda_t}(S_{t+1} + D_{t+1})\right]$. Thus far nothing is different from the baseline model in the chapter. However, the way in which the Lagrange multiplier λ_t evolves over time is now more complicated. Take the first-order condition of the Lagrangian with respect to c_t to get

$$u_1(c_t, c_{t-1}) - \lambda_t P_t + \beta u_2(c_{t+1}, c_t) = 0,$$

where the notation u_i denotes the partial derivative of the instantaneous utility function with respect to the i th argument (since the instantaneous utility function here has two arguments). Thus $u_1(c_t, c_{t-1})$ is the marginal utility in period t of period t consumption, while $u_2(c_{t+1}, c_t)$ is the marginal utility in period $t+1$ of period t consumption—that is, due to the habit persistence, period-t consumption affects utility in both periods t and $t+1$ (reflecting the "habit formation"), which must be taken into account. Solving the above for the Lagrange multiplier, we have $\lambda_t = \dfrac{u_1(c_t, c_{t-1}) + \beta u_2(c_{t+1}, c_t)}{P_t}$, and thus updating the time subscripts by one period, similarly in period $t+1$, $\lambda_{t+1} = \dfrac{u_1(c_{t+1}, c_t) + \beta u_2(c_{t+2}, c_{t+1})}{P_{t+1}}$. Inserting these two into the stock price equation above gives

$$S_t = \beta \left[\frac{u_1(c_{t+1}, c_t) + \beta u_2(c_{t+2}, c_{t+1})}{u_1(c_t, c_{t-1}) + \beta u_2(c_{t+1}, c_t)} \cdot \frac{P_t}{P_{t+1}} \left(S_{t+1} + D_{t+1} \right) \right].$$

The period-t stock price is affected by not only c_{t+1} and c_t (the standard model) but also, due to habit persistence, c_{t+2} and c_{t-1}. Thus, with habit persistence, asset prices are said to be more forward-looking as well as more backward-looking than without habits, and this idea seems to better capture empirically the behavior of stock prices than the model without habit persistence (a topic for a more advanced course in finance theory).

b. With no habits (our baseline model), the price S_t depended on period t and period $t+1$ consumption. With one lag of consumption as the habit model (part a above), the price S_t depended on period $t-1$, t, $t+1$, and $t+2$ consumption. Thus having one lag of consumption introduced one more backward-looking and one more forward-looking consumption term in the pricing equation. Adding yet one more lag to the habit model would introduce yet another backward-looking and yet another forward-looking consumption term in the pricing equation: thus, consumption in periods $t-2$, $t-1$, t, $t+1$, $t+2$, and $t+3$ would all affect the period-t stock price. And so on for even further lags of consumption in the period-t instantaneous utility function.

5. "Hyperbolic Impatience" and Stock Prices

a. The two FOCs are

$$-\lambda_t S_t + \gamma \beta \lambda_{t+1} (S_{t+1} + D_{t+1}) = 0$$
$$-\gamma \beta \lambda_{t+1} S_{t+1} + \gamma \beta^2 \lambda_{t+2} (S_{t+2} + D_{t+2}) = 0$$

b. Simply rearranging the two FOCs above and canceling the γ term (along with one β term) in the second FOC, we have

$$S_t = \frac{\gamma\beta\lambda_{t+1}}{\lambda_t}(S_{t+1} + D_{t+1})$$

$$S_{t+1} = \frac{\beta\lambda_{t+2}}{\lambda_{t+1}}(S_{t+2} + D_{t+2})$$

For the next questions, observe that the S_t expression and the S_{t+1} expression are subtly, but importantly, different here. They would be identical to each other (other than the fact that the time subscripts are different, but that is as usual) if and only if $\gamma = 1$. If $\gamma < 1$, which is the case of "hyperbolic impatience," then stock prices are determined in a somewhat "different way" in the "very short run" compared to the "longer short run" or "medium run."

For the remainder of this problem, assume that $D_{t+1} = D_{t+2}$ is known, that $S_{t+1}=S_{t+2}$, and that $\lambda_t = \lambda_{t+1} = \lambda_{t+2}$.

c. No, none of these statements necessarily implies that the economy is in a steady state, which, recall, means that all real variables become constant and never again change. There are two ways of observing that the information above does not imply the economy is in steady state. First, the statements above are all about nominal variables, and in a steady state it can be the case that nominal variables continue fluctuating over time, even though all real variables do not. Another way of arriving at the correct conclusion here is that the statements above only refer to periods t, $t+1$, and $t+2$. In a steady state, (real) variables settle down to constant values forever, not just for a few time periods.

d. You are given that nominal stock prices, nominal dividends, and the Lagrange multiplier in period $t+1$ and $t+2$ are equal to each other. Let's call these common values $\overline{S}$, $\overline{D}$, and $\overline{\lambda}$

(i.e., $\overline{S} = S_{t+1} = S_{t+2}$ $\overline{D} = D_{t+1} = D_{t+2}$, and $\overline{\lambda} = \lambda_{t+1} = \lambda_{t+2}$). Inserting these common values in the period-t+1 stock price equation, we have $\overline{S} = \dfrac{\beta\overline{\lambda}}{\overline{\lambda}}(\overline{S} + \overline{D})$. Canceling terms, we have that the nominal stock price in period t+1 (and t+2) is $\overline{S} = \beta\overline{S} + \beta\overline{D}$ (which we could of course solve for the stock price as $\overline{S} = \dfrac{\beta}{1-\beta}\overline{D}$ if we needed to).

Now using the common values of S, D, and the multiplier in the period-t stock price equation gives us $S_t = \gamma\beta(S_{t+1} + D_{t+1}) = \gamma\beta(\overline{S} + \overline{D}) = \gamma(\beta\overline{S} + \beta\overline{D})$. Note that the final term in parentheses is nothing more than $\overline{S}$; hence we have

$$S_t = \gamma\overline{S}.$$

If $\gamma < 1$, then clearly the stock price in period t is smaller than it is in period t+1 (and period t+2). The economics of this is due to the "hyperbolic impatience," which makes consumers more impatient to purchase consumption in the "very short run" (period t) compared to the "longer short run." All else equal, this means that in the very short run, consumers' do not care to save as much (due to their extreme impatience in the very short run), which means their demand for saving (i.e., their demand for stock) is lower. Lower demand for stock means a lower price of stock, all else equal.

Now also suppose that the utility function in every period is $u(c) = \ln c$, and also that the real interest rate is zero in every period.

e. This only requires examining the lifetime utility function (the first line of the Lagrangian above). By definition, the MRS between period t consumption and t+1 consumption is $\dfrac{u'(c_t)}{\gamma\beta u'(c_{t+1})} = \dfrac{c_{t+1}}{\gamma\beta c_t}$, and the MRS between period t+1 consumption and t+2 consumption is

$$\frac{\gamma\beta u'(c_{t+1})}{\gamma\beta^2 u'(c_{t+2})} = \frac{u'(c_{t+1})}{\beta u'(c_{t+2})} = \frac{c_{t+2}}{\beta c_{t+1}}$$. Note that the form of the two MRS functions is different: the

hyperbolic impatience affects the former MRS but not the latter MRS.

f. The basic consumption-savings optimality condition states that the MRS between two

consecutive time periods is equated to $(1+r)$. You are told here that $r = 0$ always. Based on

the two MRS functions constructed above, then, it follows immediately that the consumption

growth rate between period t and $t+1$ is smaller than the consumption growth rate between

period $t+1$ and period $t+2$. This follows because $\gamma < 1$. The economics is similar to above:

hyperbolic impatience makes consumers consume "much more" in the very short run (i.e.,

period t), which means that the growth rate of consumption between period t (already a very

high consumption period) and $t+1$ will be low, compared to the similar comparison one

period later.

Chapter 9 Problem Set Solutions

1. Preference Shocks in the Consumption-Savings Model

a. An increase in B means each unit of period-2 consumption delivers more utility to the consumer. Thus, in utility terms, period-2 consumption has now become more valuable relative to period-1 consumption, implying that in order to stay on a given indifference curve the consumer now needs to give up fewer units of c_2 in order to get one more unit of c_1. In a diagram with c_2 on the vertical axis and c_1 on the horizontal axis, this is represented by a flattening of the indifference map. Because the LBC is unaffected, the flattening of the indifference map means that the new optimal choice features smaller period-1 consumption and hence larger period-2 consumption, as shown in the accompanying diagram. As drawn, consumption in period 1 is smaller than real income in period 1, but that is irrelevant.

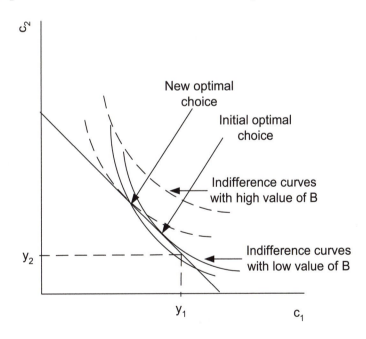

b. We can deduce the effect on private savings in period 1 using the diagram in part a above. The real interest rate has not changed (in other words, the slope of the LBC has not changed), yet the representative consumer's savings in period 1 has increased. This follows directly from the observation that income y_1 is constant while consumption in period 1 falls. This result would be true for any choice of the real interest rate (i.e., no matter the slope of the LBC); hence the private savings function shifts outward, as shown below.

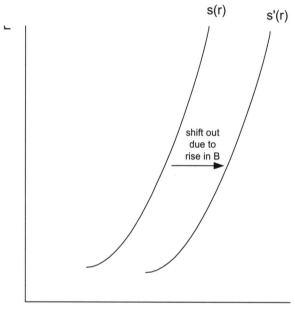

Period-1 Savings

c. Yes, these effects are consistent with developments in consumption and savings behavior in the United States leading up to the invasion of Iraq. An interpretation we can give using the model here is that consumers believed future macroeconomic conditions would be better than current (i.e., just before the war) macroeconomic conditions, hence a fall in consumption in the present (period 1) accompanied by a (expected) rise in consumption in the future (period 2). With B pre-multiplying consumption in the utility function (in the case here, period-2 consumption), the term B can be interpreted as a measure of "consumer confidence": a rise in B signals that consumers are shifting their preferences towards consumption (in that period). So here we might interpret events as consumers being more confident about the future than the present, hence they postpone some consumption until the future.

d. Setting up the Lagrangian in the two-period model as always, we have

$$\ln(c_1) + \ln(B \cdot c_2) + \lambda \left[y_1 + \frac{y_2}{1+r_1} - c_1 - \frac{c_2}{1+r_1} \right],$$

in which for simplicity we have assumed the initial assets equal zero because it does not at all affect the consumption-savings optimality condition (verify this yourself). The FOCs on c_1 and c_2 are, respectively,

$$\frac{1}{c_1} - \lambda = 0$$

$$\frac{B}{B \cdot c_2} - \frac{\lambda}{1+r_1} = 0$$

In the FOC on c_2, note that the B term ends up canceling out (recall that the derivative of an expression such as $\ln(2x)$ is $2/(2x) = 1/x$). Combining these two FOCs as usual then yields that at the optimal choice,

$$\frac{1/c_1}{1/c_2} = 1+r_1,$$

the left-hand side of which is the intertemporal MRS, as always. Note that it is independent of the preference shifter B, which turns out to be a special feature of the log utility function.

e. Here we return to a general utility specification, not necessarily log. With the utility function written as $u(Dc_1, c_2)$ and a decrease in D, the analysis above is completely unchanged. The fall in D makes consumption in period 1 less valuable in utility terms relative to period-2 consumption, which means that in order to obtain one more unit of period-2 consumption, while remaining on the same indifference curve, the consumer must give up more units of period-1 consumption than he had to before the fall in D. But in a diagram with c_2 on the vertical axis and c_1 on the horizontal axis, this simply means that the indifference curves become flatter, just as in part a.

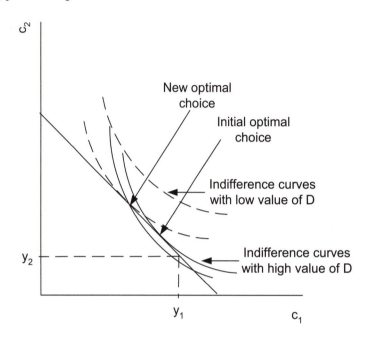

This exercise cautions you to think about the underlying economics—specifically, how the consumer's marginal rate of substitution (refer to chapter 1) is affected—when analyzing preference shocks. We cannot make a blanket statement such as "the indifference map flattens when the measure of the preference shock increases" because it depends on exactly how we introduce the preference shock into our theoretical model. Here in part d we introduced the preference shock by attaching it to period-1 consumption, whereas earlier we introduced the preference shock by attaching it to period-2 consumption.

3.   Impulse Response Function and Labor Supply: Part 2

Letting $u(c_t, n_t) = \ln(c_t - \psi \cdot n_t)$ stand for the period-t utility function, its associated marginal utility with respect to consumption and labor, respectively, are

$$u_c(c_t, n_t) = \frac{1}{c_t - \psi \cdot n_t}$$

and

$$u_n(c_t, n_t) = \frac{1}{c_t - \psi \cdot n_t} \cdot (-\psi).$$

(Recall the use of the Chain Rule of Calculus that is required for the latter FOC.) Based on the basic consumption-labor optimality condition, $-\dfrac{u_n(c_t, n_t)}{u_c(c_t, n_t)} = w_t$ (which is true for any period t as long as labor markets are perfectly competitive), inserting the marginal utilities above gives us

$$-\left(\frac{\dfrac{1}{c_t - \psi \cdot n_t} \cdot (-\psi)}{\dfrac{1}{c_t - \psi \cdot n_t}} \right) = w_t,$$

which seems to be a gigantic expression. It actually boils down quite neatly by canceling terms to

$$\psi = w_t,$$

which characterizes the labor-supply function. A natural question based on this expression is: how or why does this describe the labor-supply function?

The answer is that because n^S does not appear in this consumption-labor optimality condition at all (i.e., n^S does not depend at all on w), optimal labor supply is perfectly elastic with respect to the real wage. In a diagram with the real wage on the vertical axis and n^S on the horizontal axis, the labor supply "function" is a perfectly horizontal line.

5. Two Types of Stock

a. Setting up the sequential Lagrangian starting from period t onward is a straightforward extension of what we've seen in the chapter:

$$u(c_t) + \beta u(c_{t+1}) + \beta^2 u(c_{t+2}) + \ldots$$
$$+ \lambda_t \left[Y_t + S_t^{SP} a_{t-1}^{SP} + D_t^{SP} a_{t-1}^{SP} + S_t^{DOW} a_{t-1}^{DOW} + D_t^{DOW} a_{t-1}^{DOW} - P_t c_t - S_t^{SP} a_t^{SP} - S_t^{DOW} a_t^{DOW} \right]$$
$$+ \beta \lambda_{t+1} \left[Y_{t+1} + S_{t+1}^{SP} a_t^{SP} + D_{t+1}^{SP} a_t^{SP} + S_{t+1}^{DOW} a_t^{DOW} + D_{t+1}^{DOW} a_t^{DOW} - P_{t+1} c_{t+1} - S_{t+1}^{SP} a_{t+1}^{SP} - S_{t+1}^{DOW} a_{t+1}^{DOW} \right]$$
$$+ \ldots.$$

Taking FOCs with respect to c_t, a_t^{SP}, and a_t^{DOW} and combining these FOCs as usual yields two (very similar) stock-pricing equations:

$$S_t^{DOW} = \frac{\beta u'(c_{t+1})}{u'(c_t)} \cdot \left(S_{t+1}^{DOW} + D_{t+1}^{DOW} \right) \cdot \frac{P_t}{P_{t+1}}$$

$$S_t^{SP} = \frac{\beta u'(c_{t+1})}{u'(c_t)} \cdot \left(S_{t+1}^{SP} + D_{t+1}^{SP} \right) \cdot \frac{P_t}{P_{t+1}}$$

b. No, it is not possible to tell whether or not $S_t^{DOW} = S_t^{SP}$ simply because you are thus far given no information on the dividends that each of these two different assets pay.

Assume for the remainder of this problem that $\beta = 1$ and that Dow stock always pays *zero* dividends.

c. Recall that we can express things in terms of the MRS between period-t and period-$t+1$ consumption. Doing this using each type of stock, we have

$$\frac{u'(c_t)}{u'(c_{t+1})} = \frac{\beta(S_{t+1}^{DOW} + D_{t+1}^{DOW})}{S_t^{DOW}} \cdot \frac{P_t}{P_{t+1}}$$

and

$$\frac{u'(c_t)}{u'(c_{t+1})} = \frac{\beta(S_{t+1}^{SP} + D_{t+1}^{SP})}{S_t^{SP}} \cdot \frac{P_t}{P_{t+1}} .$$

The reason that we have two alternative ways of expressing the consumption-savings optimality condition here is simply because we are considering two alternative assets. With the assumption that $\beta = 1$, $D_{t+1}^{DOW} = 0$, $D_{t+1}^{SP} = 0.1S_{t+1}^{SP}$, and the given information $\frac{P_t}{P_{t+1}} = \frac{1}{1 + \pi_{t+1}} = \frac{1}{1.1}$, we can write the two expressions above as

$$\frac{u'(c_t)}{u'(c_{t+1})} = \frac{S_{t+1}^{DOW}}{S_t^{DOW}} \cdot \frac{1}{1.1}$$

and

$$\frac{u'(c_t)}{u'(c_{t+1})} = \frac{1.1S_{t+1}^{SP}}{S_t^{SP}} \cdot \frac{1}{1.1} .$$

Remember, a steady state means that consumption becomes constant from one period to the next. If consumption is constant from one period to the next, clearly marginal utility of consumption becomes constant from one period to the next as well, meaning the left-hand side of the last two expressions equals one in steady state:

$$1 = \frac{S_{t+1}^{DOW}}{S_t^{DOW}} \cdot \frac{1}{1.1}$$

and

$$1 = \frac{1.1S_{t+1}^{SP}}{S_t^{SP}} \cdot \frac{1}{1.1} .$$

From these two steady-state expressions, it is clear how Dow prices and S&P prices are changing over time: from the second expression, S&P prices are clearly not changing over time, whereas in the first expression, Dow prices are rising at a rate of 10 percent, the same as the rate of consumer price inflation.

The intuition behind these results is as follows. No matter which we way we measure the "real interest rate" (whether using Dow returns or S&P returns), they must both must be equal to the consumer's MRS. The Dow stock pays no dividend, hence its entire return must come through changes in the price of the stock itself—meaning there are capital gains on the Dow stock. In contrast, because S&P stocks do pay a dividend, the required capital gains on S&P stock are lower. With the particular numerical values given, the required capital gain on S&P stock turns out to be zero.

Chapter 15 Problem Set Solutions

1. Deriving a Money Demand Function

For each utility function, we have now written the marginal utility functions u_{c_t} and u_{m_t}. Also note that you are, in each question, being asked to solve for $\dfrac{M_t}{P_t}$ as a function of c_t and i_t,

which is the consumer's real money demand.

a. Constructing the consumption-money optimality condition with the given functions, we have

$$\frac{u_{m_t}}{u_{c_t}} = \frac{1/(M_t/P_t)}{1/c_t} = \frac{P_t c_t}{M_t} = \frac{i_i}{1+i_t}.$$

Solving for M_t/P_t, we have

$$\frac{M_t}{P_t} = \frac{c_t(1+i_t)}{i_t}.$$

Thus the function $\phi(\cdot)$ function is $\phi(c_t,i_t) = \dfrac{c_t(1+i_t)}{i_t}$, which is increasing in consumption

and decreasing in the nominal interest rate, as expected.

b. Proceeding as above, the consumption-money optimality condition is

$$\frac{u_m}{u_c} = \frac{1/\sqrt{M_t/P_t}}{1/\sqrt{c_t}} = \frac{\sqrt{P_t}\sqrt{c_t}}{\sqrt{M_t}} = \frac{i_t}{1+i_t}.$$

Solving for M_t/P_t, we have

$$\frac{M_t}{P_t} = \frac{c_t(1+i_t)^2}{i_t^2}$$

(be careful with the algebra here—notice the squared terms in the solution). Thus the function $\phi(\cdot)$ function is $\phi(c_t, i_t) = \dfrac{c_t(1+i_t)^2}{i_t^2}$, which is increasing in consumption and decreasing in the nominal interest rate, again as expected.

c. The consumption-money optimality condition is

$$\frac{u_m}{u_{c_t}} = \frac{1-\sigma}{\sigma} \cdot \frac{c_t^{\sigma}(M_t/P_t)^{-\sigma}}{c_t^{\sigma-1}(M_t/P_t)^{1-\sigma}} = \frac{i_t}{1+i_t}.$$

After combining exponents, we can write this as

$$\frac{1-\sigma}{\sigma} \cdot c_t \cdot \frac{P_t}{M_t} = \frac{i_t}{1+i_t}.$$

Solving for M_t/P_t, we have

$$\frac{M_t}{P_t} = \frac{1-\sigma}{\sigma} \cdot \frac{c_t(1+i_t)}{i_t}.$$

Thus, the function $\phi(\cdot)$ is

$$\phi(c_t, i_t) = \frac{1-\sigma}{\sigma} \cdot \frac{c_t(1+i_t)}{i_t}.$$

3. The Yield Curve

a. With maturity lengths plotted on the horizontal axis, the yield curve in terms of bond prices is downward-sloping. This follows simply because of the inverse relationship between bond prices and interest rates. The yield curve shown above is in terms of interest rates and is strictly increasing; hence the associated yield curve in terms of prices must be strictly decreasing.

b. The only two first-order conditions that you needed here are those on B_t and B_t^{TWO}. Denote by λ_t the Lagrange multiplier on the period-t budget constraint and by λ_{t+1} the Lagrange multiplier on the period-$t+1$ budget constraint. Then the two first-order conditions, respectively, are

$$-\lambda_t P_t^b + \beta \lambda_{t+1} = 0$$

and

$$-\lambda_t P_t^{b,TWO} + \beta^2 \lambda_{t+2} = 0.$$

Note well the $t+2$ time subscripts in the second expression; this follows from the fact the a two-period bond purchased in period t does not repay its promised face value until period $t+2$.

c. From the first expression above, we have, as usual that $P_t^b = \dfrac{\beta \lambda_{t+1}}{\lambda_t}$. From the second expression above, we analogously can obtain $P_t^{b,TWO} = \dfrac{\beta^2 \lambda_{t+2}}{\lambda_t}$. We can rewrite this expression for the price of a two-period bond as

$$P_t^{b,TWO} = \frac{\beta \lambda_{t+2}}{\lambda_{t+1}} \frac{\beta \lambda_{t+1}}{\lambda_t},$$

in which we have simply multiplied and divided the preceding expression by λ_{t+1} (i.e., we have multiplied by one, always a valid mathematical operation). The final term on the far right-hand side is nothing more than the price of a one-period bond, so we can write

$$P_t^{b,TWO} = \frac{\beta \lambda_{t+2}}{\lambda_{t+1}} P_t^b,$$

which satisfies the form of the relationship you were asked to derive. We can actually boil this down further, though. Note that the price of one-period bond purchased *in* period $t+2$ would be given by

$$P_{t+1}^b = \frac{\beta \lambda_{t+2}}{\lambda_{t+1}},$$

which follows from optimization with respect to period $t+1$ one-period bond holdings. Using this expression in the period-t price of a two-period bond, we thus obtain

$$P_t^{b,TWO} = P_{t+1}^b P_t^b,$$

which is a key idea in finance theory: the price of a multi-period asset (bond) is nothing more than the product of the prices of two consecutive one-period assets (bond).

d. Start with the relationship $P_t^{b,TWO} = \frac{\beta \lambda_{t+2}}{\lambda_{t+1}} P_t^b$ derived above. If nominal consumption expenditures are constant (and equal to one) every period, this means that $\lambda = 1$ every period. (This conclusion follows from the fact that the FOC with respect to consumption is $1/c_t - \lambda_t P_t = 0$ in every period, which can be rearranged to $\lambda_t = \frac{1}{P_t c_t}$). If the multiplier is one every period, we immediately have

$$P_t^{b,TWO} = \beta P_t^b.$$

Because $\beta < 1$, we conclude $P_t^{b,TWO} < P_t^b$.

e. Extending the Lagrangian from above, the first-order condition with respect to B_t^{THREE} is

$$-\lambda_t P_t^{b,THREE} + \beta^3 \lambda_{t+3} = 0,$$

which can be rearranged to yield $P_t^{b,THREE} = \dfrac{\beta^3 \lambda_{t+3}}{\lambda_t}$. Just like in part c above, by cleverly

multiplying by one, we can express this as

$$P_t^{b,THREE} = \frac{\beta^2 \lambda_{t+3}}{\lambda_{t+2}} \frac{\beta \lambda_{t+2}}{\lambda_{t+1}} \frac{\beta \lambda_{t+1}}{\lambda_t},$$

which, in exactly the same way as in part c, we can express in terms of chained one-period

bond prices,

$$P_t^{b,THREE} = \frac{\beta \lambda_{t+3}}{\lambda_{t+2}} P_{t+1}^b P_t^b.$$

If the Lagrange multiplier λ is constant every period, we can conclude the price of a three-

period bond is smaller than the price of a two-period bond (which in turn, from part c, is

smaller than the price of a one-period bond). This again follows because $\beta < 1$.

f. Based on the analyses in parts d and e, the price of bonds is clearly negatively-related to its

maturity length, hence the yield curve in terms of prices is strictly decreasing. This is just as

your sketch of the empirical yield curve in part a.

g. Re-examining our conclusions/analyses in parts d, e, and f, the sole reason we were able to

reach the conclusions we reached in each of those parts was the fact that $\beta < 1$. Thus the idea

of impatience and its effects on the macroeconomy rears its head again, this time with respect

to bond prices of different maturities. The conceptual idea is simple: because of impatience,

the longer a bond purchaser must wait to receive a given face value, the less he will be

willing to pay for it today (and this is reflected in bond market prices through the bond

demand function for different maturity bonds).

5. Monetary Policy in the MIU Model

a. Examining the right-hand side of the above, it is clear that the smaller is i, the flatter is the budget line. Starting from the FIXED point, draw two budget lines, with the budget line with slope i^1 flatter than the budget line with slope i^2. On the flatter budget line, the consumer's optimal choice of money balances and consumption is higher than on the steeper budget line.

b. Again as is clear from the diagram, choosing the smaller value of i allows the representative consumer to attain a higher level of utility (a higher indifference curve), so i^1 is preferred to i^2.

c. Setting $i = 0$ (or, technically speaking, very very very close to zero) would make the budget line completely flat, and allow the consumer to obtain the highest possible utility. Note that because indifference curves are downward sloping, if $i < 0$, then there would not be a point of tangency between the budget line and an indifference curve—there would no equilibrium. (Of course, $i = 0$ is the lowest that nominal interest rates can ever go (something known as the "zero-lower-bound" on interest rates—were they to go lower, a monetary economy (i.e., one in which money is used as a medium of exchange) would not exist. This is a topic for a more advanced course in monetary economics.

Chapter 16 Problem Set Questions

1. Unpleasant Monetarist Arithmetic*

Consider a finite-period economy, the final period of which is period T (so that there is no period $T+1$)—every agent in the economy knows that period T is the final period of the economy. In this economy the government conducts both fiscal policy (engaging in government spending and collecting taxes) and monetary policy (expanding or contracting the money supply). The timing of fiscal policy and monetary policy will be described further below. The economy has now arrived at the very beginning of period T, and the period-T consolidated government budget constraint is

$$M_T - M_{T-1} + B_T + P_T t_T = (1 + i_{T-1})B_{T-1} + P_T g_T,$$

where the notation is as follows:

- M_t is the nominal money supply at the end of period t;

- B_t is the nominal quantity of government debt outstanding at the end of period t (i.e., a positive value of B_t here means that the government is in debt at the end of period t);

_____

*This problem is based on a classic work in macroeconomic theory by Thomas Sargent and Neil Wallace ("Some Unpleasant Monetarist Arithmetic," *Federal Reserve Bank of Minneapolis Quarterly Review,* vol. 5, 1981).

- t_t is the real amount of lump-sum taxes the government collects in period t (and there are no distortionary taxes);

- i_{t-1} is the nominal interest rate on government assets held between period $t-1$ and t, and it is known with certainty in period $t-1$;

- g_t is the real amount of government spending in period t;

- P_t is the nominal price level of the economy in period t.

Thus, once period T begins, the economic objects yet to be determined are t_T, g_T, M_T, and B_T. How P_T is set is described more fully below.

Compute the numerical value of B_T. Show any important steps in your computations/logic.

Solution   This is simply an application of our idea that an economic agent cannot end its life with anything other than zero assets. This is because for utility-maximization purposes it would not make sense for the economic agent to die with strictly positive assets, and if everyone knows the agent will not be around in the next period to pay its debts, it cannot die with strictly negative assets (i.e., cannot die in debt). Hence we have $B_T = 0$.

The rest of this question is independent of part a. So, for the remainder of this question, suppose that for some reason $B_T = 0$—the fiscal authority is committed to this decision about bonds and will never deviate from it. Also suppose, for the remainder of this question, that $i_{T-1} = 0.10$, $B_{T-1} = 10$ (i.e., the government is in debt at the beginning of period T, by the definition of B_t), $P_{T-1} = 1$ (notice the time subscript here), and $M_{T-1} = 10$.

The timing of fiscal policy and monetary policy is as follows. At the beginning of any period t, the monetary authority and the fiscal authority independently decide on monetary policy (the choice of M_t) and fiscal policy (the choices of t_t and g_t), respectively.

Finally, in parts b and c, suppose that the nominal price level is flexible (i.e., it is not at all "sticky").

b. Suppose that the fiscal side of the government decides to run a primary real fiscal surplus of $t_T - g_T = 9$ in period T. Assume that the monetary authority chooses a value for M_T that, when coupled with this fiscal policy, implies zero inflation between period $T-1$ and period T. Compute numerically the real value of seignorage revenue the government earns in period T, clearly explaining the key steps in your computations/logic. Also provide brief economic intuition for why the government needs to generate this amount of seignorage revenue in period T?

Solution   A useful rearrangement of the government budget constraint (GBC) is

$$(1+i_{T-1})B_{T-1} = P_T(t_T - g_T) + M_T - M_{T-1}$$

in which we have imposed $B_T = 0$. A second useful way of writing this expression is

$$(1+i_{T-1})B_{T-1} = P_T\left[t_T - g_T + \frac{M_T - M_{T-1}}{P_T} \right],$$

in which we now have, as the second term inside square brackets, real seignorage revenue in period T. This expression states that the nominal value of government debt outstanding (inclusive of interest payments)—which is the left-hand side of this expression—must equal the nominal value of the fiscal surplus plus the nominal value of seignorage revenue.

If there is zero inflation between period $T-1$ and period T, then clearly $P_T = P_{T-1} = 1$. To compute real seignorage revenue, we must first find M_T, the amount of money the monetary authority decides for the end of period T. With the given values, the previous expression immediately gives us that $M_T = 12$. Real seignorage revenue in period T is thus

$$\frac{M_T - M_{T-1}}{P_T} = \frac{12-10}{1} = 2 .$$

c. Suppose that the monetary authority sticks to its monetary policy (i.e., its choice of M_t) you found in part b above. However, the fiscal authority decides instead to run a primary real fiscal surplus of $t_T - g_T = 8$. Compute numerically the real value of seignorage revenue the government must earn in period T as well as the inflation rate between period $T-1$ and period T. Clearly explain the key steps in your computations/logic. In particular, why is real seignorage revenue here different or not different from what you computed in part b?

Solution The monetary authority continues to choose $M_T = 12$, as found in part b above. The GBC, of course, must continue to hold—let's now use the first form of the GBC derived in part b. Inserting the given values, the GBC becomes $(1+0.10)10 = P_T(8) + 12 - 10$, in which the only unknown is clearly the nominal price level P_T. Thus we have $P_T = 1.125$, which means that there is 12.5 percent inflation between period $T-1$ and period T.

Real seignorage revenue is thus $\dfrac{M_T - M_{T-1}}{P_T} = \dfrac{12-10}{1.125} = 1.777$, less than the 2 units of real seignorage revenue in part b. The reason for the difference is that the price level adjusts between period $T-1$ and period T while the monetary authority sticks to a nominal policy of $M_T = 12$.

The generation of a smaller real fiscal surplus in the final period of the economy would mean it needs more real seignorage revenue if it had to repay a fixed real amount of debt. However, by generating inflation, the government is able to reduce the real amount of debt B_{T-1}/P_T it must repay, which offsets the smaller real seignorage revenue.

In part d, assume the nominal price level is "completely sticky"—that is, the nominal price level never varies from one period to the next.

d. With "complete stickiness" of the price level, is a monetary policy that sets the level of M_T you found in part b consistent with a fiscal policy that sets a real fiscal surplus of $t_T - g_T = 8$ as in part c? In other words, can those policies work simultaneously? Explain carefully why or why not, using any appropriate mathematical or logical arguments.

Solution   With complete stickiness, $P_T = P_{T-1} = 1$, since the price level never changes. The GBC then can be written as $(1+i_{T-1})B_{T-1} = t_T - g_T + M_T - M_{T-1}$. After the given values are inserted, including that $M_T = 12$ as found in part b, the right-hand side of this expression is

$$t_T - g_T + M_T - M_{T-1} = 8 + 12 - 10 = 10,$$

while the left-hand side of this expression is

$$(1+i_{T-1})B_{T-1} = 11.$$

Clearly, then, the GBC doesn't hold with equality! This means this combination of fiscal policy (i.e., $t_T - g_T = 8$) and monetary policy (i.e., $M_T = 12$) doesn't "work" together—the policies are inconsistent with each other because both do not satisfy the GBC.

e. Reviewing the scenarios posed in parts b, c, and d, address the following question in a brief discussion: what is the role of fiscal policy in determining the inflation rate and/or the nominal price level in the economy? If possible, connect your remarks to the debate between the RBC view and the New Keynesian view. (NOTE: There is no single correct answer here, but if you conducted the analysis above correctly, there is a generally correct theme that emerges. You are not simply being asked to summarize the results above but rather to try to draw some bigger picture insight.)

Solution   Picking up on the theme articulated in the last sentence of the solution in part d, the big picture issue here is that monetary policy and fiscal policy must somehow work "hand-in-hand" with each other. Thus it is not just monetary policy that determines the path of nominal prices, and hence inflation in the economy, but also fiscal policy, a point that is not appreciated enough. With flexible prices (i.e., the RBC view), the way that any arbitrary combination of fiscal policy and monetary policy is "made consistent" with each other is through completely unfettered adjustment of prices—some appropriate amount of inflation can occur through market forces to make the policies work together. However, with (completely) sticky prices, the price-adjustment mechanism is unavailable to make arbitrary combinations of fiscal and monetary policy consistent with each other—in this case it is incumbent on the fiscal and/or monetary authorities to react to each other's policy choices to make them consistent with each other. Under the New Keynesian view, in which prices are sticky but not completely unchangeable, we would obtain an intermediate result—the price-adjustment mechanism works to partially make arbitrary fiscal and monetary policies consistent with each other, but it is also partially incumbent on the policy makers to make them consistent. Note that the ideas developed here, while having nothing to do with our study of exchange rates, are reminiscent of our "fiscal theory of exchange rates" and directly to our look at monetary-fiscal interactions. Recall that one broad theme emerged there: that fiscal policy and monetary policy somehow had to be "consistent" with each other in order for a fixed exchange rate system to work in the long run. Here we see that "consistency" between monetary policy and fiscal policy is a deeper issue throughout macroeconomics, not just exchange rate determination.

2. The Dynamics of Fiscal Policy

President Obama and his primary economic advisers put in place large fiscal stimuli in early 2009. In early 2009 the precise details of the fiscal stimulus were still to be worked out, but they included tax cuts as well as increased government spending in the next few years.

It is early 2009, and the new administration has just recently been seated. At the beginning of 2009, the lifetime consolidated budget constraint of the government was

$$
\frac{B_{2008}}{P_{2009}} = (t_{2009} - g_{2009}) + \frac{t_{2010} - g_{2010}}{1 + r_{2010}} + \frac{t_{2011} - g_{2011}}{(1 + r_{2010})(1 + r_{2011})} + \frac{t_{2012} - g_{2012}}{(1 + r_{2010})(1 + r_{2011})(1 + r_{2012})} \cdot
$$

$$
+ sr_{2009} + \frac{sr_{2010}}{1 + r_{2010}} + \frac{sr_{2011}}{(1 + r_{2010})(1 + r_{2011})} + \frac{sr_{2012}}{(1 + r_{2010})(1 + r_{2011})(1 + r_{2012})} + ...
$$

Line 1: PDV of fiscal deficits

Line 2: PDV of seignorage

The notation here is as in chapter 15: t denotes real lump-sum tax collections, g denotes real government spending, sr denotes real seignorage revenue, r denotes the real interest rate, B denotes nominal (one-period) government bonds, and P denotes the nominal price level of the economy (i.e., the nominal price of one basket of consumption). Subscripts indicate time periods, which we will consider to be calendar years. Note, of course, the ellipsis (…) in each line of the equation above.

As indicated in the equation, the first line of the right-hand side is the present discounted value of all fiscal deficits the government will ever run starting from 2009 onward, and the second line of the right-hand side is the present-discounted value of all seignorage revenue that will ever result from the monetary policy actions of the Federal Reserve starting from 2009 onward.

The primary economic advisers to President Obama are Treasury Secretary Timothy Geithner, National Economic Council Chairman Lawrence Summers, and Council of Economic Advisers Chairwoman Christina Romer.

In addressing each of the following issues, no quantitative work is required at all; the following questions all require only conceptual analysis. Each issue should be addressed in no more than three or four sentences.

Geithner, because of his background as president of the New York Federal Reserve, implicitly advocates that no matter what fiscal policy actions the new administration takes, they should be designed in such a way as to have no effects whatsoever on the conduct of monetary policy. If this is so, what type of fiscal policy—a Ricardian fiscal policy or a non-Ricardian fiscal policy—does Geithner advocate? Briefly explain.

Solution   The policy is Ricardian because it is being conducted in a way to ensure that tax revenues and/or government spending adjust (in a PDV sense) to, by themselves, ensure lifetime government budget balance.

a. The less even-keeled that he is, Summers' comments sometimes seem to imply that the fiscal stimulus measures should not take into account any consequences they might have for the conduct of monetary policy. If the combination of tax cuts and government spending that ultimately pan out over the next few years follow Summers' advice, what are likely to be the consequences for the Federal Reserve's monetary policy in 2009 and beyond? In particular, will the Fed likely have to expand or contract the nominal money supply? Briefly explain.

Solution   By lowering the PDV of fiscal surpluses (i.e., increasing the PDV of fiscal deficits) and given a fixed B/P (if you assumed this, this is fine; if they made some more sophisticated argument (i.e., FTPL) as to why B/P may NOT be fixed, then will need to trace through that argument), the PDV of seignorage revenue must rise to balance the lifetime government budget constraint. Increased seignorage requires an increase (at some point) in the nominal money supply.

a.   The objective academic macroeconomist that she is, Romer typically points outs in her remarks that because fiscal policy plans (for both taxes and government spending) will almost surely be revised as the years unfold (i.e., fiscal policy plans adopted in 2009 can be revised in later years), it may be impossible to know beforehand what the eventual consequences for monetary policy of a particular fiscal policy action adopted at the start of 2009 might be. Use the government budget constraint presented above to interpret what Romer's statements mean.

Solution   The interpretation is that economic events unfold over time and that, perhaps most important, economic shocks, by their very definition, are not known until they occur. One of many examples is an unpredicted government spending shock that occurred in 2012 and has lasted for many years. In 2009, this shock was not foreseen, but, starting in 2012, the lifetime consolidated government budget constraint will look different (perhaps dramatically so). As of

2009, what then will be the eventual (i.e., starting in 2009) consequences be for monetary

policy? It's impossible to say, because the 2012 shock was unpredicted.

a. If, later in 2009 after the new fiscal plans are (supposedly) clarified further, the nominal price

level of the economy behaves as shown in the following diagram (the price level, P, is

plotted on the vertical axis), which of the following is the most relevant explanation: the

fiscal theory of the price level, or the fiscal theory of inflation? Briefly justify your answer.

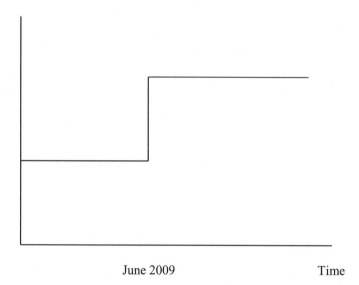

June 2009   Time

Solution   This illustrates the FTPL because there is a one-time jump in P (at the time of the

fiscal reform).

3.   Greece and Long-Run Fiscal (In)Solvency

The current European economic and sovereign debt crisis has put into sharp focus one of the

main challenges of enacting a single currency zone (the eurozone, or the euro area, as it is

officially called) and hence a single monetary policy among (17) sovereign countries, but

without enacting a single fiscal policy across those countries. Consider specifically the case of

Greece, which is the most highly indebted country (in terms of percentage of its GDP—the

Greek government's debt is roughly 150 percent of Greek GDP) in the euro area. (Throughout

the rest of this problem, the terms "single-currency zone," "eurozone," and "euro area" are used

interchangeably.)

In this problem, you will apply the Fiscal Theory of the Price Level (FTPL) studied in

chapter 16 to the analysis of fiscal policy in a single-currency zone. In studying or applying the

FTPL, the condition around which the analysis revolves is the present-value (lifetime)

consolidated government budget constraint (GBC). Recall that starting from the beginning of

period t, the present-value consolidated GBC is

$$\frac{B_{t-1}}{P_t} = \sum_{s=0}^{\infty} \frac{t_{t+s} - g_{t+s}}{\prod_{x=1}^{s}(1 + r_{t+x-1})} + \sum_{s=0}^{\infty} \frac{sr_{t+s}}{\prod_{x=1}^{s}(1 + r_{t+x-1})},$$

in which all of the notation is just as in chapter 16.

You are given three numerical values. First, suppose that $B_{t-1} = €340$ billion (which

roughly corresponds to what the Greek government's total nominal debt is at present). Second,

assume that $t_t - g_t = - €20$ billion (note the minus sign—this value roughly corresponds to

Greece's fiscal balance in the third quarter of 2011). Third, the Greek nominal price level in

period $t - 1$ is $P_{t-1} = 1$ (which is a normalization).

Due to its high indebtedness, Greece was under the specter of default and possible exit

from the single-currency zone. To avoid these dramatic adverse consequences, Greece was

compelled (by other European governments) to make strict fiscal adjustments as well as other

reforms to stabilize the rapid increase in government debt.

(NOTE: In some of the analysis below, you will need to make use of the geometric summation result from basic mathematics. Here is a brief description of the geometric summation result. Suppose that a variable x is successively raised to higher and higher powers, and the infinite sequence of these terms is summed together, as in

$$x^0 + x^1 + x^2 + x^3 + x^4 + ...$$
$$= \sum_{s=0}^{\infty} x^s$$

in which the second line compactly expresses the infinite summation using the summation notation Σ. This sum can be computed in a simple way according to

$$\sum_{s=0}^{\infty} x^s = \frac{1}{1-x}.$$

This expression is the geometric summation result, which you studied in a pre-calculus or basic calculus course and which you will need to apply in some of the analysis below.)

General Solution   In much of the analysis below, you needed to apply the geometric summation result. This result applies here because all of the economic terms (specifically, $t - g$ and sr) in the present value GBC do not depend on the index of summation s and thus can be pulled outside the summation operator. In other words, this is essentially a steady-state analysis. The present value GBC can thus be simplified to

$$B_{t-1} = (t-g) \sum_{s=0}^{\infty} \frac{1}{(1+r)^s} + sr \sum_{s=0}^{\infty} \frac{1}{(1+r)^s},$$

which can be simplified even further. The two key observations you had to make were the following. First, the term $\dfrac{1}{(1+r)^s}$ can be expressed as $\left(\dfrac{1}{1+r}\right)^s$ by the rule of exponents. Second, in terms of the general form of the geometric summation given above, the variable "x" corresponds to the term $\dfrac{1}{1+r}$. Applying the geometric summation result, we have

$$\sum_{s=0}^{\infty}\left(\frac{1}{1+r}\right)^s = \frac{1}{1-\dfrac{1}{1+r}} = \frac{1}{\dfrac{1+r-1}{1+r}} = \frac{1}{\dfrac{r}{1+r}} = \frac{1+r}{r}.$$

With this, the present-value GBC is expressed as

$$B_{t-1} = \left(\frac{1+r}{r}\right)(t-g) + \left(\frac{1+r}{r}\right)sr,$$

or, equivalently,

$$B_{t-1} = \left(\frac{1+r}{r}\right)(t-g+sr).$$

The entire analysis is then based on either of these last two representations of the present-value GBC, which from here we will refer to as the PVGBC.

a. In a single-currency zone (e.g., the euro area), monetary policy is carried out by a "common" central bank (the European Central Bank in the euro area). A consequence of this is that individual countries—in particular, Greece—cannot print their own money (despite the fact that there is a Bank of Greece). What is the implication of this for Greece's seignorage revenue? And, how would this impact Greece's present-value GBC? Explain as clearly as possible, including, if needed, any mathematical analysis.

Solution: Not being allowed to print nominal money means $M_t - M_{t-1} = 0$ in every period t, which in turn means (by definition) that seignorage revenue is $sr_t = \dfrac{M_t - M_{t-1}}{P_t} = 0$ in every period. The present-value GBC (PVGBC) then is simply

$$\frac{B_{t-1}}{P_t} = \sum_{s=0}^{\infty} \frac{t_{t+s} - g_{t+s}}{\prod_{s=1}^{\infty}(1 + r_{t+s})}.$$

The real value of government liabilities thus has to be financed by pure fiscal surpluses.

b.   Suppose that Greece commits to stay in the single-currency zone and to carry out all necessary fiscal adjustments to ensure its present-value GBC is satisfied. Suppose that the real interest rate is constant in every period at 5 percent ($r = 0.05$) and that the nominal price level in period t will remain $P_t = 1$ (note this is the period-t price level, not the period-t–1 price level).[†] Suppose Greece carries out its fiscal adjustments in period t, and (to simplify things a bit) Greece will keep the new fiscal surplus (or fiscal deficit) constant at that level in all subsequent time periods. What is the numerical value of the fiscal surplus (or fiscal deficit) in order to ensure that the present-value consolidated GBC from part a is satisfied? That is, what is the numerical value of $(t - g)$? Be clear about the sign and the numerical

---

[†]And note that what is relevant here is the real interest rate, not the nominal interest rate, which had shot up in Greece to about 25 percent in October 2011. The reason why real interest rates, not nominal rates, matter most directly is that markets' expectations of inflation for Greece (if Greece did indeed exit from the eurozone) was near 20 percent.

magnitude of $(t - g)$. Present your economic and/or mathematical logic; and provide brief economic explanation.

Solution   Using the given numerical values in the PVGBC, write

$$\frac{340 \text{ billion}}{1} = \frac{B_{t-1}}{P_t} = \left(\frac{1+0.05}{0.05}\right)(t-g) \text{ ,}$$

from which it obviously follows that $(t - g) = 16.19$ billion. Intuitively, if the entire debt has to be repaid using a constant fiscal surplus (and zero seignorage) over time, that surplus has to $16.19 billion in every time period.

Re-do the analysis in part b, assuming instead that $r = 0.025$. Compare the conclusion here with the conclusion in part b, providing brief economic explanation for why the conclusions do or do not differ.

Solution   Using the given numerical values in the PVGBC, write

$$\frac{340 \text{ billion}}{1} = \frac{B_{t-1}}{P_t} = \left(\frac{1+0.025}{0.025}\right)(t-g) \text{ ,}$$

from which it obviously follows that $(t - g) = 8.29$ billion. Intuitively, if the entire debt has to be repaid using a constant fiscal surplus (and zero seignorage) over time, that surplus has to $8.29 billion in every time period. The required surplus in this case is smaller than in part b because of the lower interest rate, which in turn implies smaller interest payments on the debt that has to be repaid.

d. Under a more realistic view, suppose that Greece still commits to stay in the single-currency zone and to make some, but not all, of the required fiscal adjustments that you computed in part b (perhaps because of "political constraints" that we are leaving outside the analysis). To make it concrete, suppose that Greece is able to run a fiscal surplus of only €5 billion in every period (i.e., $t - g = €5$ in every time period). If the real interest rate is 5 percent ($r = 0.05$), compute the numerical value of P_t to ensure that the present-value consolidated GBC is satisfied. Be clear about your logic and computation to arrive at the result, and provide a brief economic explanation.

Solution   Using the given numerical values in the PVGBC,

$$\frac{340 \text{ billion}}{P_t} = \frac{B_{t-1}}{P_t} = \left(\frac{1+0.05}{0.05}\right) \cdot 5 ,$$

which now has to be solved for P_t. Solving this for P_t, we have

$$P_t = \frac{B_{t-1}}{\left(\dfrac{1+0.05}{0.05}\right) \cdot 5}$$

or $P_t = 3.24$. Intuitively, if the fiscal surplus cannot be as large as computed in part b and the nominal government debt is fixed at $B_{t-1} = 340$ (and $sr = 0$ always), then the only way for the PVGBC to be satisfied is for the price level to adjust (higher) in the short run. This makes the real value of the government debt to be smaller than $B_{t-1} = 340$.

e.   Redo the analysis in part d, assuming instead that $r = 0.025$. Compare the conclusion here with the conclusion in part d, providing brief economic explanation for why the conclusions do or do not differ.

Solution   Using the given numerical values in the PVGBC, write

$$\frac{340 \text{ billion}}{P_t} = \frac{B_{t-1}}{P_t} = \left(\frac{1+0.025}{0.025}\right) \cdot 5$$

which now has to be solved for P_t. Solving this for P_t obtains

$$P_t = \frac{B_{t-1}}{\left(\dfrac{1+0.025}{0.025}\right) \cdot 5}$$

or $P_t = 1.66$. Intuitively, if the fiscal surplus cannot be as large as computed in part c and the nominal government debt is fixed at $B_{t-1} = 340$ (and $sr = 0$ always), then the only way for the PVGBC to be satisfied is for the price level to adjust (higher) in the short run. This makes the real value of the government debt to be smaller than $B_{t-1} = 340$, but not as small as in the case computed in part d.

f. Assume that Greece decides (against the collective wisdom of other European governments) to leave the single-currency zone. Once having left the eurozone, instead of making a serious fiscal adjustment, Greece prefers to cover its debt burden through seignorage revenue, while keeping the fiscal balance unchanged (in every time period into the future) at $t - g = -$ €20 billion (note the minus sign). Suppose that the required seignorage revenue is kept at the same level in all subsequent years, and assume that $r = 0.05$ (which suppose cannot be affected by monetary policy). Address the following three questions:

i.   How much (per-period) seignorage revenue would Greece need to generate in order to keep its prices at $P = 1$ in period t and for every period beyond t?

ii. What are the implications of this particular monetary and fiscal (and, ultimately, political) policy on Greece's own future (i.e., period t and beyond) inflation rate?

iii. What is the theoretical difference between the analysis in this question and the analysis conducted in parts b and c, and with the analysis conducted in parts d and e?

Solution   If the fiscal balance is kept at a deficit (of 20 billion), then the per-period seignorage revenue needed to balance the PVGBC and keep $P = 1$ in every period requires computing seignorage revenue from

$$\frac{340 \text{ billion}}{P_t} = \frac{B_{t-1}}{P_t} = \left(\frac{1+0.05}{0.05}\right) \cdot (-20 + sr)$$

(note the -20 on the right-hand side is the per-period fiscal deficit). Solving this for sr gives

$$sr = \left(\frac{0.05}{1+0.05}\right)\frac{B_{t-1}}{P_t} - (t - g) \quad,$$

or $sr = 36.19$ in every period, which answers part i.

If Greece does actually implement and stick with this policy, then inflation will always be zero (i.e., $P = 1$ for every period into the future), which answers part ii. BUT (and this is the key part of the question—as was assumed at the start of part f) Greece is now printing its own currency because it has left the euro currency.

Finally, the analytical difference is simply that we are now allowing for the possibility that seignorage revenue will be generated by Greece due to its creation of its money, which answers part iii.

4. Inflationary Finance and Long-Run Fiscal Solvency in the United States (circa 2010)

In studying the fiscal theory of inflation (FTI) and the fiscal theory of the price level (FTPL), the condition around which the analysis revolves is the present-value (lifetime) consolidated government budget constraint (GBC). As studied in chapter 16, starting from the beginning of period t, the present-value consolidated GBC is

$$\frac{B_{t-1}}{P_t} = \sum_{s=0}^{\infty} \frac{t_{t+s} - g_{t+s}}{\prod_{s=1}^{\infty}(1 + r_{t+s})} + \sum_{s=0}^{\infty} \frac{sr_{t+s}}{\prod_{s=1}^{\infty}(1 + r_{t+s})},$$

in which all of the notation is just as in chapter 16.

Let's leave aside the FTPL, which makes a very sharp prediction about when the inflationary consequences of government indebtedness may occur (the FTPL predicts these consequences occur "immediately"). That leaves us with the FTI if we are concerned about understanding the inflationary consequences of government indebtedness. Unfortunately, the FTI makes no sharp prediction whatsoever about when any inflationary consequences of government indebtedness may occur, only predicting that it must occur at some time if the fiscal side of the government does not conduct tax policy and government spending policy appropriately.

In this problem you will study a steady-state version of the FTI, which enables the FTI to generate some long-run predictions about the inflationary consequences of government indebtedness. To operationalize the steady-state version of the FTI, suppose the following:

- The real interest rate is constant at the same value from period t onward. That is,

$r_t = r_{t+1} = r_{t+2} = r_{t+3} = ... = r > 0$ (i.e., steady state). However, the numerical value of r is left unspecified here.

- The fiscal side of the government (i.e., Congress/Treasury) always has the same fiscal surplus/deficit from period t onward. That is,

$$t_t - g_t = t_{t+1} - g_{t+1} = t_{t+2} - g_{t+2} = t_{t+3} - g_{t+3} = \ldots = t - g$$ (i.e., steady state). However, the numerical value of $t - g$ (and even whether $t - g$ is zero, positive, or negative) is left unspecified here.

- The monetary side of the government (i.e., the Federal Reserve) always collects the same seignorage revenue from period t onward. That is, $sr_t = sr_{t+1} = sr_{t+2} = sr_{t+3} = \ldots = sr$ (i.e., steady state). However, the numerical value of sr (and even whether sr is zero, positive, or negative) is left unspecified here.

- The monetary side of the government (i.e., the Federal Reserve) always expands the nominal money supply at the same rate from period t onward. That is, $\mu_t = \mu_{t+1} = \mu_{t+2} = \mu_{t+3} = \ldots = \mu$ (i.e., steady state). However, the numerical value of μ (and even whether μ is zero, positive, or negative) is left unspecified here.

- Suppose that $P_t = 1$ and does not change under any circumstances (this assumption effectively allows us to leave aside the FTPL, as stated above). (NOTE: This assumption does not necessarily imply that P_{t+1} or P_{t+2} or P_{t+3}, etc., are equal to one.)

With these steady-state assumptions, the present-value consolidated GBC from above simplifies considerably, to

$$B_{t-1} = \sum_{s=0}^{\infty} \frac{t-g}{(1+r)^s} + \sum_{s=0}^{\infty} \frac{sr}{(1+r)^s}.$$

You are given two numerical values. First, you are given $B_{t-1} = \$14 \text{ trillion}$, which roughly corresponds to what the US government's total nominal debt is at present. Second, you are given the steady-state value of real money balances, which equals \$2 trillion in every time period. That is, $\dfrac{M_t}{P_t} = \dfrac{M_{t+1}}{P_{t+1}} = \dfrac{M_{t+2}}{P_{t+2}} = \dfrac{M_{t+3}}{P_{t+3}} = ... = \$2 \text{ trillion}$ (and this roughly corresponds to what the value of

M1 money in the US economy was at the end of the year 2010).

Finally, in some of the analysis, you will need to make use of the geometric summation result from basic mathematics. Again, here is a brief description of the geometric summation result: suppose that a variable x is successively raised to higher and higher powers, and the infinite sequence of these terms is summed together, as in

$$x^0 + x^1 + x^2 + x^3 + x^4 + ...$$
$$= \sum_{s=0}^{\infty} x^s$$

in which the second line compactly expresses the infinite summation using the summation notation Σ. This sum can be computed in a simple way according to

$$\sum_{s=0}^{\infty} x^s = \frac{1}{1-x} .$$

This expression is the geometric summation result (which you studied in a pre-calculus or basic calculus course and will need to apply in some of the analysis).

General Solution   In all of the analysis, you needed to apply the geometric summation result. This result applies here because all of the economic terms (specifically, $t - g$ and sr) in the present-value GBC do not depend on the index of summation s and thus can be pulled outside the summation operator. That is, the present-value GBC can be simplified to

$$B_{t-1} = (t-g) \sum_{s=0}^{\infty} \frac{1}{(1+r)^s} + sr \sum_{s=0}^{\infty} \frac{1}{(1+r)^s} .$$

Then the two key observations you had to make were the following. First, the term $\frac{1}{(1+r)^s}$ can be expressed as $\left(\frac{1}{1+r}\right)^s$ by the rules of exponents. Second, in terms of the general form of the geometric summation given above, the variable x corresponds to the term $\frac{1}{1+r}$. Applying the geometric summation result, we have

$$\sum_{s=0}^{\infty} \left(\frac{1}{1+r}\right)^s = \frac{1}{1 - \frac{1}{1+r}} = \frac{1}{\frac{1+r-1}{1+r}} = \frac{1}{\frac{r}{1+r}} = \frac{1+r}{r} .$$

With this, the present-value GBC is expressed as

$$B_{t-1} = \left(\frac{1+r}{r}\right)(t-g) + \left(\frac{1+r}{r}\right)sr ,$$

or, equivalently,

$$B_{t-1} = \left(\frac{1+r}{r}\right)(t-g+sr) .$$

The entire analysis is then based on either of these last two representations of the present-value GBC, which from here we will refer to as the PVGBC.

Suppose that seignorage revenue will be always be zero ($sr = 0$ in every time period). If the real interest rate is 5 percent ($r = 0.05$), compute the numerical value of $(t-g)$ that the fiscal side of the government must set in every time period to ensure that the present-value consolidated GBC is satisfied. (Be clear about the sign and the magnitude.) Present your logic, and provide brief economic explanation.

Solution Using the given numerical values in the PVGBC, write

$$14 \text{ trillion} = B_{t-1} = \left(\frac{1+0.05}{0.05}\right)(t-g) ,$$

from which it obviously follows that $(t-g) = \dfrac{2}{3}$ trillion $= 667$ billion. Intuitively, if the entire debt has to be repaid using a constant fiscal surplus (and zero seignorage) over time, that surplus has to $667 billion in every time period.

Re-do the analysis in part a, assuming instead that $r = 0.025$. Compare the conclusion here with the conclusion in part a, providing brief economic explanation for why the conclusions do or do not differ.

Solution Using the given numerical values in the PVGBC, write

$$14 \text{ trillion} = B_{t-1} = \left(\frac{1+0.025}{0.025}\right)(t-g) ,$$

from which it obviously follows that $(t-g) = 0.3415$ trillion $= 341.5$ billion. Intuitively, if the entire debt has to be repaid using a constant fiscal surplus (and zero seignorage) over time, that surplus has to $341.5 billion in every time period. The required surplus in this case is much smaller than in part a because of the lower interest rate, which implies smaller interest payments on the debt that has to be repaid.

Suppose that the fiscal side of the government is able to balance its budget in every period ($t - g = 0$ in every time period), but (perhaps because of political considerations) is never able to run a surplus (but also never runs a deficit). If the real interest rate is 5 percent ($r = 0.05$) and assuming that r cannot be affected by monetary policy, compute the numerical value of sr that the monetary side of the government must generate in every time period to ensure the present-value consolidated GBC is satisfied. (Be clear about the sign and the magnitude.) Present your logic, and provide brief economic explanation.

Solution   Using the given numerical values in the PVGBC, write

$$14 \text{ trillion} = B_{t-1} = \left(\frac{1+0.05}{0.05} \right) sr ,$$

from which it obviously follows that $sr = \dfrac{2}{3}$ trillion $= 667$ billion . Intuitively, if the entire debt has to be repaid using a constant quantity of seignorage revenue over time (because $t\text{-}g = 0$ in every time period), seignorage revenue has to $667 billion in every time period.

Re-do the analysis in part c, assuming instead that $r = 0.025$. Compare the conclusion here with the conclusion in part c, providing brief economic explanation for why the conclusions do or do not differ.

Solution   Using the given numerical values in the PVGBC, write

$$14 \text{ trillion} = B_{t-1} = \left(\frac{1+0.025}{0.025} \right) sr ,$$

from which it obviously follows that $sr = 0.3415$ trillion $= 341.5$ billion . Intuitively, if the entire debt has to be repaid using a constant quantity of seignorage revenue over time (because $t\text{-}g = 0$ in every time period), seignorage revenue has to $341.5 billion in every time period. As in part b, the required seignorage revenue is much smaller than in part c because of the lower interest rate, which implies smaller interest payments on the debt that has to be repaid.

In order to generate the amount of seignorage revenue you computed in part c, what money growth rate μ will the Federal Reserve have to set? And, as a consequence, what will the inflation rate be? Present your logic, and provide brief economic explanation.

Solution   The starting point of the analysis here was the definition of seignorage revenue: in any period t, $sr_t = \dfrac{M_t - M_{t-1}}{P_t}$ (which is simply a definition). Re-expressing this slightly is helpful:

$$sr_t = \frac{M_t - M_{t-1}}{P_t} = \frac{M_t}{P_t} - \frac{M_{t-1}}{P_t} = \frac{M_t}{P_t} - \frac{M_{t-1}}{P_{t-1}}\frac{P_{t-1}}{P_t} = \frac{M_t}{P_t} - \frac{M_{t-1}}{P_{t-1}}\frac{1}{1+\pi_t}.$$

The second equality follows from breaking apart the fraction; the third equality follows from multiplying and dividing by P_{t-1}; and the third equality follows from the definition of inflation.

Next you are told that seignorage revenue is identical in every time period and that real money balances are equal to $2 trillion in every time period; it thus follows that

$$sr = 2 - \frac{2}{1+\pi_t}.$$

The final key analytic observation is that in the steady state, the money growth rate equals the inflation rate, $\mu = \pi$ (recall this result from chapter 14), coupled with the given assumption the money growth rate is identical in every time period. The previous expression then becomes

$$sr = 2 - \frac{2}{1+\mu} = 2\left(1 - \frac{1}{1+\mu}\right) = 2\left(\frac{1+\mu-1}{1+\mu}\right) = 2\left(\frac{\mu}{1+\mu}\right).$$

In part c we found that the required seignorage revenue was 667 billion = (2/3) trillion. Hence we need to solve the expression

$$sr = \frac{2}{3} = 2\left(\frac{\mu}{1+\mu}\right).$$

Straightforward algebra thus gives that the money growth rate must be $\mu = 0.50$ —that is, a 50 percent nominal money expansion in every period, which implies 50 percent inflation rate in every period.

In order to generate the amount of seignorage revenue you computed in part d, what money growth rate μ will the Federal Reserve have to set? And, as a consequence, what will the inflation rate be? Present your logic, and provide brief economic explanation.

Solution Using identical analysis as in part e, we need to solve the expression

$$sr = 0.3415 \text{ trillion} = 2\left(\frac{\mu}{1+\mu}\right).$$

Straightforward computation gives that that the money growth rate must be $\mu = 0.2059$ —that is, a roughly 20 percent nominal expansion in every period, which implies a roughly 20 percent inflation rate in every period.

Unlike some countries' central banks, in 2010, the US Federal Reserve did not have an inflation rate that they "officially" were "required" to conduct policy with a goal towards attaining. However, the "informal" inflation goal of the Federal Reserve at the time seemed to be 2 percent a year. If the real interest rate is 5 percent ($r = 0.05$), and assuming that r cannot be affected by monetary policy, compute the numerical value of $(t - g)$ that the fiscal side of the government must set in every time period to ensure the present-value consolidated GBC is satisfied provided that the Fed will always attain its 2 percent inflation target. (Be clear about the sign and the magnitude.) Present your logic, and provide brief economic explanation.

Solution From the analysis and discussion in part e, we know that $sr = 2\left(\dfrac{\mu}{1+\mu}\right) = 2\left(\dfrac{\pi}{1+\pi}\right)$.

Supposing that the Fed always maintains 2 percent inflation ($\pi = 0.02$), we have $sr = 0.0392$ trillion (don't lose track of the units here).

Next examine the PVGBC. With this level of seignorage revenue and a 5 percent real interest rate, the PVGBC is

$$14 = B_{t-1} = \left(\frac{1+0.05}{0.05}\right)(t-g) + \left(\frac{1+0.05}{0.05}\right)0.0392 \text{ ,}$$

which we simply have to solve for $t - g$. Computing this, we have $t - g = 0.6275$ trillion; that is, the fiscal surplus must be \$627.5 billion in every period. Notice this is slightly smaller than the fiscal surplus computed in part a, which is because in the analysis here there is some positive seignorage revenue being earned; in part a, seignorage revenue was zero.

Re-do the analysis in part g, assuming instead that $r = 0.025$. Compare the conclusion here with the conclusion in part g, providing brief economic explanation for why the conclusions do or do not differ.

Solution Following the same logic as above, we have

$$14 = B_{t-1} = \left(\frac{1+0.025}{0.025}\right)(t-g) + \left(\frac{1+0.025}{0.025}\right)0.0392 \text{ .}$$

Solving this for the fiscal surplus in every period, we have $t - g = 0.3022$ trillion, that is, $302.2 billion. This is substantially smaller than in part g because of the smaller interest payments on the debt that has to be repaid.

Chapter 17 Problem Set Solutions

1. Evaluating the Welfare of Various Policies

a. With this utility function, the marginal utility functions are $u_1(c, 1-n) = 1/c$ and

$u_2(c, 1-n) = 1/(1-n)$. (Note that there is no minus sign for $u_2(.)$! The second argument of

the function $u(.)$ is leisure, which is the entire term $1-n$. Computing $u_2(.)$ means

computing the marginal utility *of leisure*—i.e., $u_2(.)$ is not the derivative with respect to n,

it is the derivative with respect to the entire term $1-n$...). Using these marginals in the

expression that compresses the description of the entire equilibrium (i.e., the private-sector

equilibrium reaction function), and recalling that in this model $c = n$ always (due to the

resource constraint), we can solve

$$\frac{\overline{c}}{1-\overline{c}} = \frac{1+g}{1+g+1+g-\beta}$$

for steady-state consumption $\overline{c}$. After a couple of steps of algebra, we have

$$\overline{c} = \frac{1+g}{3(1+g)-\beta},$$

which simply shows us how steady-state equilibrium consumption depends on the discount

factor and the money growth rate. It is easy to compute that for $g = -0.04$, $g = 0$, and

$g = 0.04$, the steady-state levels of consumption are, respectively, $\overline{c} = 0.5000$, $\overline{c} = 0.4902$,

and $\overline{c} = 0.4815$. Inserting these steady-state equilibrium values back into the utility function

shows us that the realized steady-state utilities of the three different policies are, respectively,

$u(0.5000, 1-0.5000) = -1.3863$, $u(0.4902, 1-0.4902) = -1.3867$, and

$u(0.5200, 1 - 0.5200) = -1.3877$.[‡] Thus, the policy $g = 0.04$ delivers the lowest welfare (utility), and the policy $g = -0.04$ delivers the highest welfare. Of course, we already knew that $g = -0.04$ would deliver the highest welfare—that's simply the Friedman rule ($g = \beta - 1$), which we have analytically proved to be the optimal (i.e., maximizes welfare) policy. (Also, of course, the utility values themselves do not have any meaning to them—all we use them for is to rank utility.)

b. As we just computed above, clearly the steady-state level of consumption declines the higher is the money growth rate. The intuition behind this result is that higher money growth, because it causes higher inflation, makes consumption more costly relative to leisure because consumers must accumulate an asset (money) whose value erodes more quickly because of inflation in order to consume. Inflation (higher money growth) induces a substitution away from those activities that require cash-holdings (here, consumption) and into those activities that do not require cash-holdings (here, leisure).

3.   Consumption as a Function of the Money Growth Rate

What you are being asked to do is come up with the function $\overline{c}(g)$, then examine its derivative to see if it can ever be zero. To obtain $\overline{c}(g)$, use the condition

---

[‡]Actually steady-state utility are these values divided by $1 - \beta$ because really what we (the policy maker) is interested in (presumably) is lifetime utility, and dividing by $1 - \beta$ puts things in terms of lifetime utility (think infinite-geometric series here). However, obviously dividing each value by $1 - \beta$ is not going to change our rankings of the different policies.

$$\frac{u_2(\bar{c}, 1 - \bar{c})}{u_1(\bar{c}, 1 - \bar{c})} = \frac{1 + g}{1 + g + 1 + g - \beta},$$

inserting the given utility function. With the given additively separable logarithmic utility function, $u_1(.) = 1/\bar{c}$, and $u_2(.) = 1/(1 - \bar{c})$. Plug these into the steady-state equilibrium reaction function, and solve for $\bar{c}$; what you get after a few steps of algebra is

$$\bar{c}(g) = \frac{1 + g}{3(1 + g) - \beta}.$$

This, of course, is identical to what we did in question 1 above. Proceeding by using the product rule obtains

$$\bar{c}'(g) = \frac{1}{3(1 + g) - \beta}\left[1 - \frac{3(1 + g)}{3(1 + g) - \beta}\right].$$

The only way this can equal zero is if the second term in the square brackets equals one. For this to occur, we need to have $\beta = 0$. But if consumers care *at all* about the future, this cannot be (i.e., $\beta = 0$ means consumers *completely* discount the future so that they don't care at all about the future). So, at least for the additively separable logarithmic utility function, it is not possible to have $\bar{c}'(g) = 0$. Clearly, this is not a way to implement the optimal policy.

Chapter 18 Problem Set Solutions

1. Graphical Representation of Economic Efficiency

The resource constraint defines a linear (with slope -1) function over c and leisure $(1 - n)$. The economically efficient outcome is that combination of c and $(1 - n)$ such that the representative consumer's MRS between consumption and leisure equals one. That is, at the economically-efficient outcome, an indifference curve of the representative consumer is tangent to the resource constraint, *not necessarily to the representative consumer's budget constraint* (which you are not given in this problem anyway).

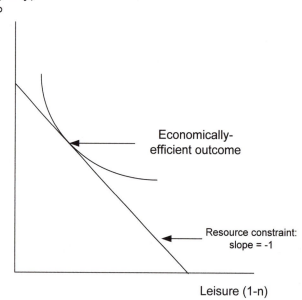

Chapter 19 Problem Set Solutions

1. The Laffer Curve

a. We have $u_1 = 1/\sqrt{c}$ and $u_2 = 1$, meaning $\sqrt{1-t}\sqrt{n} = 1-t$. Solving this for labor, we have

$$n(t) = 1-t,$$

which means that

$$TR(t) = t \cdot (1-t).$$

To determine whether a Laffer effect is present, compute

$$TR'(t) = 1-t+t \cdot (-1) = 1-2t.$$

Clearly, if $t = 0.5$, TR reaches a maximum; hence for this utility function a Laffer effect arises.

b. We have $u_1 = 1/c$ and $u_2 = 1/(1-n)$, meaning $\dfrac{(1-t)n}{1-n} = 1-t$. Solving this for labor, we have

$$n = 0.5,$$

which is completely independent of the labor tax rate! That is, no matter the tax rate, the representative consumer works 0.5 units of time. In turn,

$$TR(t) = t \cdot (0.5).$$

To determine whether a Laffer effect is present, compute

$$TR'(t) = 0.5,$$

which shows that tax revenues are always increasing in the tax rate. That is, because labor is completely unresponsive to the tax rate (in mathematical terms, $n'(t) = 0$ here), no matter how high the tax rate, if the government raises the tax rate even more it leads to more tax revenue. This point follows immediately by observing the tax revenue function here is a strictly increasing function with respect to the tax rate.

Chapter 21 Problem Set Solutions

1. Stock, Bonds, "Bills," and the Financial Accelerator

a. The Lagrangian, which by now should be extremely straightforward to construct, is

$$P_1 f(k_1, n_1) + P_1 k_1 + (S_1 + D_1)a_0 + B_0 - P_1 w_1 n_1 - P_1 k_2 - S_1 a_1 - P_1^b B_1$$
$$+ \frac{P_2 f(k_2, n_2)}{1+i} + \frac{P_2 k_2}{1+i} + \frac{(S_2 + D_2)a_1}{1+i} + \frac{B_1}{1+i} - \frac{P_2 w_2 n_2}{1+i} - \frac{P_2 k_3}{1+i} - \frac{S_2 a_2}{1+i} - \frac{P_2^b B_2}{1+i}$$
$$+ \lambda \left[R^S S_1 a_1 + R^B P_1^b B_1 - P_1 (k_2 - k_1) \right]$$

b. Based on Lagrangian above, the FOC with respect to B_1 is

$$-P_1^b + \frac{1}{1+i} + \lambda R^B P_1^b = 0.$$

c. As discussed in the chapter, financing constraints are said to "not matter" (in the context of the accelerator framework) when the value of the Lagrange multiplier is zero, $\lambda = 0$. Inserting this value for the multiplier in the FOC derived in part b, we have that

$$P_1^b = \frac{1}{1+i}.$$

Keeping in mind that in this problem we are distinguishing between i and i^{BOND}, this last expression can be written as

$$\frac{1}{1+i^{BOND}} = \frac{1}{1+i},$$

from which it is obvious that $i = i^{BOND}$. Thus, in "normal economic conditions" (i.e., when $\lambda = 0$), the nominal interest rates on "Treasury bills" and "Treasury bonds" are exactly equal.

This analytical result in fact justifies the usual practice of treating all bonds as "the same"—in normal economic conditions, their interest rates are (roughly) equalized. (Indeed, if we introduced even longer maturity bonds into our framework—two-period bonds, three-period bonds, five-period bonds, etc.—we would be led to same conclusion, that all of their interest rates are equal to each other, provided that financing constraints don't affect macroeconomic outcomes—although "impatience" introduces another caveat into this, but we have ignored impatience issues in this problem.)

d. From the FOC on B_1 computed in part b, and now without imposing $\lambda = 0$, we can perform the following algebraic rearrangements:

$$-P_1^b + \frac{1}{1+i} + \lambda R^B P_1^b = 0$$

$$\lambda = \left[P_1^b - \frac{1}{1+i} \right] \cdot \frac{1}{R^B P_1^b}$$

$$\lambda = \left[1 - \frac{1}{P_1^b} \frac{1}{1+i} \right] \cdot \frac{1}{R^B}$$

$$\lambda = \left[1 - \frac{1+i^{BOND}}{1+i} \right] \cdot \frac{1}{R^B}$$

$$\lambda = \left[\frac{1+i-(1+i^{BOND})}{1+i} \right] \cdot \frac{1}{R^B}$$

$$\lambda = \left[\frac{i-i^{BOND}}{1+i} \right] \cdot \frac{1}{R^B}$$

This final expression shows that if financing constraints "matter" (which means that $\lambda \neq 0$), then clearly $i \neq i^{BOND}$. Without knowing more about "how" financial market conditions are affecting investment behavior—that is, whether financing conditions are "tight" or "loose" (which would govern the sign of the multiplier λ), it is impossible to say anything more about how the T-bill interest rate and the T-bond interest rate compared to each other. But, regardless, it is clear that it is not appropriate to consider the two interest rates as being identical in this case.

The preceding analysis was framed in terms of nominal interest rates; the remainder of the analysis is framed in terms of real interest rates.

$$\lambda = \left[\frac{i - i^{BOND}}{1+i} \right] \cdot \frac{1}{R^B}$$

and rewrite it as

$$\lambda = \left[\frac{1 + i - (1 + i^{BOND})}{1+i} \right] \cdot \frac{1}{R^B}.$$

Next multiply and divide the term inside square brackets by $(1 + \pi)$ (which, of course, simply means that we're multiplying by one):

$$\lambda = \left[\frac{\dfrac{1+i}{1+\pi} - \dfrac{1 + i^{BOND}}{1+\pi}}{\dfrac{1+i}{1+\pi}} \right] \cdot \frac{1}{R^B}$$

By the Fisher relation, we can express this as

$$\lambda = \left[\frac{1 + r - (1 + r^{BOND})}{1 + r} \right] \cdot \frac{1}{R^B},$$

or, finally,

$$\lambda = \left[\frac{r - r^{BOND}}{1 + r} \right] \cdot \frac{1}{R^B},$$

which is obviously similar to the type of condition we derived in chapter 21 regarding stock financing.

f. The expression derived in part e and all expressions feature λ on the left-hand side. We can thus obviously set them equal to each other, giving us

$$\left[\frac{r - r^{STOCK}}{1 + r} \right] \cdot \frac{1}{R^S} = \left[\frac{r - r^{BOND}}{1 + r} \right] \cdot \frac{1}{R^B}.$$

Although you did not have to perform the next algebraic step (i.e., you could conduct the ensuing logical analysis based just on this last expression), we can multiply this entire expression through by $1+r$ and then also multiply the entire expression by R^S, which would give us

$$r - r^{STOCK} = (r - r^{BOND}) \cdot \frac{R^S}{R^B}.$$

It is obvious what the consequence of $r = r^{STOCK}$ is. If $r = r^{STOCK}$, it must also be that $r = r^{BOND}$ (because you are told that R^S cannot be zero).

Thus, if the returns on stocks ("risky assets") are equal to the return on physical assets (r), the return on bonds ("safe financial assets") are also equal to the return on physical assets (r).

This is essentially just a statement of the Fisher relation—recall from chapter 14 that one way to understand/interpret the Fisher equation is that it says the returns on "safe" and "risky" assets are equal to each other (the "no-arbitrage" relationship). Here the underlying view is that the returns on all types of bonds are "riskless" ("safe"), just as are the returns on physical capital.

g. As discussed in the chapter, one way of offsetting the feedback effects of a decline in financial market returns is to relax financial market regulations—increasing R^S and/or R^B in this case. The reason this may be helpful is that, all else equal, it would serve to lower λ (examine the conditions derived above), which is, analytically, where the problems can be traced to (i.e., the fact that financing constraints "matter"). From the financing constraint itself, it is obvious that raising R^S and/or R^B increases the "effective" market value of firms' collateralizeable financial assets (recall the basic information asymmetry problems that underlie this financing constraint):

$$P_1 \cdot (k_2 - k_1) = R^S \cdot S_1 \cdot a_1 + R^B \cdot P_1^b \cdot B_1.$$

That is, raising R^S and/or R^B increases the right-hand side of the financing constraint. But if that is infeasible for institutional or political other reasons, another policy intervention that has the same effect is to try to raise **any** of the other components of the right-hand side of the financing constraint: including government efforts to try to raise the price of bonds by directly buying them in markets (i.e., the increased demand for bonds in bond markets should, all else equal, raise the price of bonds).

This is beyond the scope of this question, but this type of analysis can shed light on a host of policy proposals and programs that are being/have been discussed the past year: many of them share the broad goal of trying to raise the "effective" market value of the private sector's collateralizeable financial assets. This could be achieved by some combination of direct government purchases of a variety of financial assets (stocks, bonds), simply "giving" firms "more assets" (i.e., directly giving them more a and/or more B), allowing "new types" of financial assets to be used for collateral purposes (i.e., adding a third asset to the right-hand side of the financing constraint, a fourth asset to the right-hand side of the financing constraint, etc.): broadly speaking, it's all about raising the right-hand side of the financing constraint above!

3. The Long Run Real Interest Rate

a. The FOCs are

$$u'(c_t) - \lambda_t - \phi_t = 0$$
$$-\lambda_t + \beta\lambda_{t+1}(1+r_{t+1}) + \beta\phi_{t+1}(1+r_{t+1}) = 0.$$
$$\beta u'(c_{t+1}) - \beta\lambda_{t+1} - \beta\phi_{t+1} = 0$$

b. An economic steady state is a condition in which all prices and quantities that are measured in real terms (i.e., in units of the aggregate consumption basket) become constant (stop fluctuating from one time period to the next).

c. Imposing steady state on the FOC on a_t requires dropping all the time subscripts since every object in the expression is a real object. Dropping time subscripts gives us

$$\lambda = \beta\lambda(1+r) + \beta\phi(1+r)$$

Divide this expression by λ and then divide the resulting expression by β, which gives

$$\frac{1}{\beta} = 1 + r + \frac{\phi}{\lambda}(1+r) = (1+r)\left(1 + \frac{\phi}{\lambda}\right)$$

(the term following the second equals sign simply groups terms together; you did not have to group terms this way).

Clearly, if $\phi = 0$, then we get the "usual" steady-state relationship $\frac{1}{\beta} = 1 + r$. However, if $\phi \neq 1$, the relationship is not satisfied. Broadly, the reason is that the "usual" relationship is predicated on the view that, at least in the long run (i.e., the steady state), credit restrictions do not affect consumption purchases (even though they may in the short run, i.e., before the steady state is reached).

If credit restrictions do affect consumption purchases in the long run, "how severely" the credit restrictions affect choices (which is captured by the multiplier ϕ) alter the relationship between market returns $1+r$ and impatience β. (We will study long-run distortions imposed on the economy by imperfect competition in financial markets later in the semester.)

d. To answer this question, start by inspecting the credit restriction and the budget constraint for period t. Given zero assets at the beginning of period t, combining the period-t budget constraint and credit constraint leads to the conclusion

$$a_t = 0.$$

Then repeat this argument for period $t+1$ (i.e., combine the period-$t+1$ budget constraint and credit constraint, now using $a_t = 0$); this leads to the conclusion that

$$a_{t+1} = 0 \, .$$

Replicating this argument forward leads to the conclusion that asset holdings at the end of every period are zero, including in the steady state.

You are asked about savings (a flow), not asset holdings per se (an accumulation variable). In any given period, savings is defined as the change in asset holdings during the course of that period—clearly, savings equals zero, in every time period, including in the steady state.

5. Optimal Tax Policy

Note for use below that we can express the second equation above as

$$w = \frac{mpn}{1 - monpol} \, .$$

The first logical step in the argument is the observation that there is *no* monopoly power if markets are perfectly competitive (by definition, obviously), in which case *monpol* = 0. In this case, we have that *mpn* = *w*. Putting this conclusion together with the consumption-leisure optimality condition gives us

$$\frac{u_l(c,l)}{u_c(c,l)} = (1-t)mpn$$

.

By the basic theory of perfect competition, you had to then recognize (implicitly or explicitly) that any tax rate different from zero creates a "wedge" (i.e., a deadweight loss) in the labor market. Hence since perfect competition means *zero* deadweight losses, the optimal tax

policy in the case of *monpol* = 0 is *t* = 0. This implies that in perfect competition, it must be that

$$\frac{u_l(c,l)}{u_c(c,l)} = mpn \, .$$

Now let's generalize the argument for the case of *monpol* > 0. Inserting the expression

$$w = \frac{mpn}{1 - monpol}$$

into the consumption-leisure optimality condition, we have

$$\frac{u_l(c,l)}{u_c(c,l)} = \frac{(1-t)mpn}{1 - monpol} \, .$$

The goal of tax policy now is to pick a *t* so that the perfect-competition outcome

$$\frac{u_l(c,l)}{u_c(c,l)} = mpn$$

is achieved despite the fact that *monpol* > 0. Examining the previous condition, it is clear that

setting *t* = *monpol* achieves the perfect-competition outcome.

Thus the optimal labor-income tax rate is *t* = *monpol*.

Chapter 22 Problem Set Solutions

1. **Symmetric Equilibrium, Real Wages, and Optimal Fiscal Policy in the Dixit-Stiglitz Model**

a. To easily compute the MRT (for any economy), construct a function based on the resource constraint, which here would be $G(c,l) = c - (1-l)$. (Note that because we are trying to construct the MRT between consumption and *leisure*, we've written this function in terms of *l*, rather than in terms of *n*.) The MRT between consumption and leisure is thus simply $G_2(.)/G_1(.)$. The required partial derivatives are obviously $G_1(.) = 1$ and $G_2(.) = 1$; hence the economy's MRT between consumption and leisure is 1. Recall the very important point that the concept of MRT, and hence its computation, has nothing whatsoever to do with firms, prices, or equilibrium. MRT is a statement purely about what the economy as a whole can achieve—that is, MRT is a statement about the resource constraint, aka production possibilities frontier, of an economy.

b. Now we are turning to consider the equilibrium of the economy. The argument here is simply a logical one. As discussed in chapter 22, because production of each unit of output requires one unit of input (labor), and labor is hired at the going market real wage w, the cost of producing one additional (i.e., the marginal) unit of output is simply w. Thus $mc = w$ in this simple economy.

c. Recall the constant-markup-pricing outcome (expressed in nominal terms) for wholesale firm j, which is $P_j = \varepsilon P mc$. The concept of symmetric equilibrium requires that $P_j = P$. Imposing this in the constant-markup-pricing rule gives us that in a symmetric equilibrium, $1 = \varepsilon mc$. On rearranging, marginal cost turns out to be (again, in a symmetric equilibrium)

104

$$mc = \frac{1}{\varepsilon},$$

which is a value < 1 due to the fact that (in a monopolistic or monopolistically-competitive environment) $\varepsilon > 1$. (Note that in the limiting case $\varepsilon = 1$, which is in fact perfect competition, we would have $mc = 1$.)

Because we concluded in part b above that $mc = w$, it furthermore is the case that (again, in a symmetric equilibrium)

$$w = \frac{1}{\varepsilon},$$

which is a value < 1 because $\varepsilon > 1$.

d. With $t = 0$, we know from above that consumer optimization yields

$$\frac{u_2(c, 1-n)}{u_1(c, 1-n)} = w.$$

We also just concluded that $w = 1/\varepsilon < 1$. Thus in equilibrium (i.e., considering both the supply and the demand sides simultaneously) we have

$$\frac{u_2(c, 1-n)}{u_1(c, 1-n)} = \frac{1}{\varepsilon}.$$

Is this the outcome a Social Planner would choose for the economy? The answer is no. The Social Planner (whose choices for the economy are, by construction, the economically efficient ones) would want to achieve

$$\frac{u_2(c, 1-n)}{u_1(c, 1-n)} = 1,$$

because the MRT between consumption and leisure in this economy is 1, as we found in part a above. Thus, at a zero tax rate, the private-sector equilibrium is not economically efficient because MRS = MRT is not attained.

e. If the labor income tax rate were $t \neq 0$, then in the private-sector equilibrium (because it is still the case that $w = 1/\varepsilon$ irrespective of what the tax rate is) we have

$$\frac{u_2(c,1-n)}{u_1(c,1-n)} = \frac{1-t}{\varepsilon}.$$

In order for economic efficiency to be achieved, the right-hand side of this expression must be set equal to one; the tax rate t can be set in such a way to achieve this. Specifically, if we want $\frac{1-t}{\varepsilon} = 1$, solving for t gives us

$$t = 1 - \varepsilon.$$

This tax rate is the optimal labor income tax rate in the presence of monopolistic competition in the goods markets. It is the "optimal" tax rate in the sense that by setting it, the private sector of the economy achieves the same exact c and l quantities that a Social Planner would achieve; thus setting $t = 1 - \varepsilon$ achieves economy efficiency.

Let's note a couple of things about this optimal tax rate. First, if perfect competition exists in the goods markets ($\varepsilon = 1$), the optimal tax rate is $t = 0$. No taxes are needed to "correct distortions" in perfectly competitive markets because perfectly competitive markets feature no distortions to begin with.

Second, with monopolistic competition, the fact that $\varepsilon > 1$ means that the optimal labor tax rate is $t < 0$. That is, the optimal labor tax rate is actually a labor subsidy! The logic behind this is the following. A monopolistic firm, because it exploits its pricing power to set a price above marginal cost, ends up producing smaller than the economically efficient quantity of goods. This in turn means that smaller than the economically efficient quantity of inputs (here, labor) is used. The government can offset this latter effect by subsidizing workers' wages—a negative labor income tax rate—which encourages them to supply more labor. If set in exactly the right way—in our framework, $t = 1 - \varepsilon$ — the government can induce the labor market to churn out exactly the economically efficient quantity of labor. Then, because the production function is simply $y = n$, the economically efficient quantity of output of goods follows.

An important broad lesson that emerges is that fiscal policy has an important role to play if markets are monopolistically competitive; under an ideal, optimal, macroeconomic policy, fiscal policy can and should offset the distortions stemming from monopolistic competition. Note that this is not monetary policy we're talking about here. The fact that fiscal policy has an important role to play if markets are monopolistically competitive will be a point that rears its head again when we consider optimal monetary policy in chapter 24.

Chapter 24 Problem Set Solutions

1. **Sticky Prices, Price Indexation, and Optimal Long-Run Inflation Targets**

a. Wholesale (intermediate) firm j's problem is a dynamic one because the nominal price it sets in any given period affects profits in the subsequent period. Written in two-period form (since that is all that is necessary for the Rotemberg problem) starting from period t, the profit function is

$$
P_{jt}y_{jt} - P_t mc_{jt}y_{jt} - \frac{\psi}{2}\left(\frac{P_{jt}}{P_{jt-1}(1+\pi)^\chi}-1\right)^2 P_t + \frac{\beta}{1+\pi_{t+1}}\left[P_{jt+1}y_{jt+1} - P_{t+1}mc_{t+1}y_{jt+1} - \frac{\psi}{2}\left(\frac{P_{jt+1}}{P_{jt}(1+\pi)^\chi}-1\right)^2 P_{t+1}\right]
$$

The objective is thus to maximize discounted profits subject to the sequence of demand functions it knows it faces in every period,

$$
y_{jt} = \left(\frac{P_{jt}}{P_t}\right)^{-\varepsilon} y_t .
$$

b. Substituting the demand function into the objective function, we have

$$
P_{jt}\left(\frac{P_{jt}}{P_t}\right)^{\frac{\varepsilon}{1-\varepsilon}} y_t - P_t mc_{jt}\left(\frac{P_{jt}}{P_t}\right)^{\frac{\varepsilon}{1-\varepsilon}} y_t - \frac{\psi}{2}\left(\frac{P_{jt}}{P_{jt-1}(1+\pi)^\chi}-1\right)^2 P_t
$$

$$
+ \frac{\beta}{1+\pi_{t+1}}\left[P_{jt+1}\left(\frac{P_{jt+1}}{P_{t+1}}\right)^{\frac{\varepsilon}{1-\varepsilon}} y_{t+1} - P_{t+1}mc_{t+1}\left(\frac{P_{jt+1}}{P_{t+1}}\right)^{\frac{\varepsilon}{1-\varepsilon}} y_{t+1} - \frac{\psi}{2}\left(\frac{P_{jt+1}}{P_{jt}(1+\pi)^\chi}-1\right)^2 P_{t+1}\right]
$$

The FOC of this problem with respect to P_{jt} is (the algebra is virtually identical to that presented in chapter 22, so refer there for details)

$$\frac{1}{1-\varepsilon} P_{jt}^{\frac{\varepsilon}{1-\varepsilon}} P_t^{\frac{\varepsilon}{\varepsilon-1}} y_t - \frac{\varepsilon}{1-\varepsilon} P_{jt}^{\frac{2\varepsilon-1}{1-\varepsilon}} P_t^{\frac{2\varepsilon-1}{\varepsilon-1}} mc_t y_t - \psi \left(\frac{P_{jt}}{P_{jt-1}(1+\pi)^\chi} -1 \right) \frac{P_t}{P_{jt-1}(1+\pi)^\chi} + \frac{\beta\psi}{1+\pi_{t+1}} \left(\frac{P_{jt+1}}{P_{jt}(1+\pi)^\chi} -1 \right) \frac{P_{t+1}}{P_{jt}(1+\pi)^\chi} \frac{P_{jt+1}}{P_{jt}} = 0$$

c. Following the same several steps of algebra as presented in chapter 22 (except now, of course, including the indexation term), we get

$$\frac{1}{1-\varepsilon}\left[1-\varepsilon mc_t\right] y_t - \psi \left(\frac{P_t}{P_{t-1}(1+\pi)^\chi} -1 \right) \frac{P_t}{P_{t-1}(1+\pi)^\chi} + \frac{\beta\psi}{1+\pi_{t+1}} \left(\frac{P_{t+1}}{P_t(1+\pi)^\chi} -1 \right) \frac{P_{t+1}}{P_t(1+\pi)^\chi} \frac{P_{t+1}}{P_t} = 0$$

By the definition of inflation, this can be expressed as

$$\frac{1}{1-\varepsilon}\left[1-\varepsilon mc_t\right] y_t - \psi \left(\frac{1+\pi_t}{(1+\pi)^\chi} -1 \right) \left(\frac{1+\pi_t}{(1+\pi)^\chi} \right) + \beta\psi \left(\frac{1+\pi_{t+1}}{(1+\pi)^\chi} -1 \right) \left(\frac{1+\pi_{t+1}}{(1+\pi)^\chi} \right) = 0,$$

which is the NKPC modified to allow for price indexation.

d. We can drop the time subscripts to get the steady-state version of the NKPC,

$$\frac{1}{1-\varepsilon}\left[1-\varepsilon mc\right] y - \psi \left(\frac{1+\pi}{(1+\pi)^\chi} -1 \right) \left(\frac{1+\pi}{(1+\pi)^\chi} \right) + \beta\psi \left(\frac{1+\pi}{(1+\pi)^\chi} -1 \right) \left(\frac{1+\pi}{(1+\pi)^\chi} \right) = 0,$$

or, combine exponents,

$$\frac{1}{1-\varepsilon}\left[1-\varepsilon mc\right] y - \psi \left((1+\pi)^{1-\chi} -1 \right)(1+\pi)^{1-\chi} + \beta\psi \left((1+\pi)^{1-\chi} -1 \right)(1+\pi)^{1-\chi} = 0$$

Solving this for *mc,* we have, after several steps of algebra,

$$mc = \frac{1}{\varepsilon} + \frac{\varepsilon-1}{\varepsilon} \frac{\psi(1-\beta)}{\varepsilon y} \left((1+\pi)^{1-\chi} -1 \right)(1+\pi)^{1-\chi}$$

e. Simply examining the steady state expression derived in part d, if $\chi = 1$, which means that $(1+\pi)^{1-\chi} = 0$, immediately implies that $mc = 1/\varepsilon$, exactly the same as in the baseline flexible-price Dixit-Stiglitz framework. The interpretation of this is that full indexation, on average, fully removes the consequences of price rigidities. This idea is intuitive—if firms can and do costlessly adjust their nominal prices at the same rate as average inflation, then, on average, the costs of price adjustment have no consequence. We have already illustrated this in the context of the Rotemberg model, where the analytics are a bit easier than in the Calvo or Taylor models, but the same result obtains in these latter models.

f. If the goal is to get to $mc = \dfrac{1}{\varepsilon}$, then obviously, in the case of less than full indexation, setting $\pi = 0$ achieves that outcome (simply examine the expression derived in part d above).

Thus we have the optimal monetary policy prescription from any baseline sticky-price model—set a long-run inflation target of zero, which is indeed the result we obtained in chapter 23. In the formalities of the Rotemberg model, this implies there are zero costs of nominal price adjustment. But, once again, this result is more general and applies in any sticky-price model; in the formalities of the Calvo model (as well as the Taylor model), a zero inflation policy eliminates nontechnologically warranted price dispersion across firms/sectors of the economy.

g. With $\chi = 1$, examination of the NKPC provides no guidance as to what the optimal long-run inflation rate should be—simply because any rate of inflation is consistent with the flexible-price outcome anyway. Hence we need to look to other possible monetary frictions in the economy—for example, if there are important money demand distortions (e.g., modeled in a CIA or MIU fashion), that would recommend the Friedman rule as the optimal monetary policy. The main message here is that with full price indexation, price-setting frictions are completely eliminated in the long-run and hence cannot be the basis/justification for offering long-run inflation policy recommendations.

3. Optimal Monetary Policy in Cash Good/Credit Good Model

a. The sequential formulation of the Lagrangian is

$$u(c_{1t}, c_{2t}) + \beta u(c_{1t+1}, c_{2t+1}) + \beta^2 u(c_{1t+2}, c_{2t+2}) + \ldots$$
$$+ \lambda_t \left[P_t y_t + M_{t-1} + \tau_t - P_t c_{1t} - P_t c_{2t} - M_t \right]$$
$$+ \mu_t \left[M_t - P_t c_{1t} \right]$$
$$+ \beta \lambda_{t+1} \left[P_{t+1} y_{t+1} + M_t + \tau_{t+1} - P_{t+1} c_{1t+1} - P_{t+1} c_{2t+1} - M_{t+1} \right]$$
$$+ \beta \mu_{t+1} \left[M_{t+1} - P_{t+1} c_{1t+1} \right]$$
$$+ \ldots$$

The first-order conditions with respect to c_{1t}, c_{2t}, M_t are, respectively,

$$u_1(c_{1t}, c_{2t}) - \lambda_t P_t - \mu_t P_t = 0$$
$$u_2(c_{1t}, c_{2t}) - \lambda_t P_t = 0$$
$$-\lambda_t + \mu_t + \beta \lambda_{t+1} = 0$$

b. To help us compute the MRT, define a function $G(c_1, c_2) = 1.2 c_1 + c_2 - y$, which, of course, is simply the resource constraint. That is, you're asked to compute the ratio of partials, G_2 / G_1, which has units cash goods per credit good. The reason G_2 / G_1 is cash goods per credit goods is that the units of G_2 is "output per credit good" and the units of G_1 is "output per cash good"; canceling units, G_2 / G_1 thus measures, from the Social Planner's standpoint, cash goods per credit good. Computing $G_2 / G_1 = 1/1.2$ obtains the required MRT.

c. We know that economic efficiency occurs when MRS = MRT. We computed the MRT above, $G_2 / G_1 = 1/1.2$. For economic efficiency, we are thus trying to solve for the money growth rate that sets

$$\frac{u_2}{u_1} = \frac{1+g}{2+2g-\beta} = \frac{1}{1.2} = \frac{G_2}{G_1}.$$

A couple of steps of algebra allows us to find that $g = \frac{\beta}{0.8} - 1$ is the optimal money growth rate.

d. Clearly, the policy found in part c is not the Friedman rule (the Friedman rule is $g = \beta - 1$). Compared to the policy in part c, for the Friedman rule the optimal policy here is to have a money growth rate higher than $g = \beta - 1$. The reason that the government wants to not deflate as fast as the Friedman rule is that there is a technological difference between cash goods and credit goods here—that is, unlike our study in chapter 20, their MRT is not one. When the MRT between cash and credit goods is not one, economic efficiency requires something other than the Friedman rule.

Chapter 25 Problem Set Solutions

1. Comparative Statics in the Solow Model

a.

$$\frac{\partial \ln k^*}{\partial \ln s} = \frac{1}{1-\alpha} \cdot \frac{1}{s} > 0$$

b.

$$\frac{\partial \ln k^*}{\partial \ln \delta} = -\frac{1}{1-\alpha} \cdot \frac{1}{(1+gr_X)\cdot(1+gr_N)-(1-\delta)} < 0$$

c.

$$\frac{\partial \ln k^*}{\partial \ln \alpha} = -\frac{1}{(\alpha-1)\cdot(\alpha-1)} \cdot \ln\left[\frac{(1+gr_X)\cdot(1+gr_N)-(1-\delta)}{s}\right]$$

d.

$$\frac{\partial \ln k^*}{\partial \ln gr_X} = \frac{1}{\alpha-1} \cdot \frac{1+gr_N}{(1+gr_X)\cdot(1+gr_N)-(1-\delta)} > 0$$

e.

$$\frac{\partial \ln k^*}{\partial \ln gr_N} = \frac{1}{\alpha-1} \cdot \frac{1+gr_X}{(1+gr_X)\cdot(1+gr_N)-(1-\delta)} > 0$$

Chapter 27 Problem Set Solutions

1. Search, Unemployment, and Matching

a. The FOC with respect to c is $\dfrac{1}{c} - \lambda = 0$.

b. The FOC with respect to n^s is

$$-\frac{1}{\left(1-p^{FIND}\right)s+n^s} + \lambda \cdot p^{FIND} \cdot (1-t) \cdot w - \mu = 0 .$$

(Note carefully the negative sign.)

c. The FOC with respect to s is (be careful to use the Chain Rule here!)

$$-\frac{1-p^{FIND}}{\left(1-p^{FIND}\right)s+n^s} + \lambda \cdot \left(1-p^{FIND}\right) \cdot b + \mu \cdot p^{FIND} = 0 .$$

(Caution: All of the remaining parts of problem 1 are based on the optimality condition obtained here in part d.)

d. After several steps of algebra to eliminate the two Lagrange multipliers λ and μ, we have

$$\frac{\dfrac{1}{\left(1-p^{FIND}\right)\cdot s+n^s}}{1/c} = p^{FIND} \cdot (1-t) \cdot w + \left(1-p^{FIND}\right) \cdot b .$$

This is the "consumption-labor optimality condition," in which the MRS is displayed on the left-hand side and the "relative price" is displayed on the right-hand side.

NOTE: This was not needed in the solutions, but this may help shed further light on the left-hand side "MRS." Suppose that we were not given the particular utility functional form

$\ln c - \ln\left(\left(1 - p^{FIND}\right) \cdot s + n^s\right)$, and instead the just described representative individual's utility

function $u\left(c, \left(1 - p^{FIND}\right) \cdot s + n^s\right)$. There are two arguments in this function, separated by a

comma. Going through steps a, b, c, and d, the final solution would be

$$-\frac{u_2\left(c, \left(1 - p^{FIND}\right) \cdot s + n^s\right)}{u_1\left(c, \left(1 - p^{FIND}\right) \cdot s + n^s\right)} = p^{FIND} \cdot (1-t) \cdot w + \left(1 - p^{FIND}\right) \cdot b$$

which shows that the left-hand side is indeed the MRS between the "pair of goods" in the

utility function.

e. Inserting $p^{FIND} = 1$ in the consumption-labor optimality condition from part d, we get

$$\frac{1/n^s}{1/c} = (1-t) \cdot w \quad.$$

Using the "NOTE" from part d above, we see that

$$-\frac{u_2\left(c, n^s\right)}{u_1\left(c, n^s\right)} = (1-t)w \quad.$$

f. Inserting $b = 0$ in the consumption-labor optimality condition from part d, we get

$$\frac{\dfrac{1}{\left(1 - p^{FIND}\right) \cdot s + n^s}}{1/c} = p^{FIND} \cdot (1-t) \cdot w \quad.$$

For the remainder of problem 1, return to the case that $p^{FIND} < 1$ and $b > 0$.

The US Bureau of Labor Statistics' (BLS) definition of "labor force participation" is

$$lfp = (1 - p^{FIND})s + n^s.$$

g. Substituting the definition of *lfp* into the optimality condition from part d gives

$$\frac{c}{lfp} = p^{FIND} \cdot (1-t) \cdot w + \left(1 - p^{FIND}\right) \cdot b$$

.

h. Slightly rewriting the right-hand side (which you were not required to do) yields

$$\frac{c}{lfp} = p^{FIND} \left[(1-t) \cdot w - b\right] + b,$$

which is slightly easier to understand if we're thinking in terms of the diagram requested. This expression clearly shows that there is a negative relationship between p^{FIND} and *lfp*.

i. For a given unit of time spent outside the labor force, a lower chance of being able to successfully find a job would increase the incentive to enter the pool of actively-searching unemployed people (i.e., to enter *s*, or more broadly, *lfp*—it was fine if it was stated in either way).

j. The expression in part h (or, if you prefer, the expression in part g, which are exactly the same expression, just slightly rewritten) shows that if *b* increases, the diagram in part h would *shift* rightward. (It would be a shift because *b* does not appear on either the vertical axis or on the horizontal axis.)

k. The economics is that for any given job-finding probability p^{FIND}, more generous unemployment benefits for those do not successfully find a job would induce more people to join the *s* pool of individuals (or, more broadly, the labor force).

3. Consumption, Labor, and Unemployment: Fiscal Policy Choices in a Search Framework

a. Start by substituting the time constraint $n = 1 - l$ into the given budget constraint, which gives

$$c + s(1-l) = p^{FIND}(1-t)w(1-l) + \left(1 - p^{FIND}\right)bl.$$

The next goal is to group together all the terms involving l. Expanding out terms on both the left-hand and right-hand sides gives

$$c + s - sl = p^{FIND}(1-t)w - p^{FIND}(1-t)wl + \left(1 - p^{FIND}\right)bl.$$

Then grouping terms involving l on the right-hand side together gives

$$c + s - sl = p^{FIND}(1-t)w - \left[p^{FIND}(1-t)w - \left(1 - p^{FIND}\right)b \right]l.$$

After moving the term in square brackets over to the left-hand side, and grouping it together with the $-sl$ term on the left-hand side, we have

$$c + \left[p^{FIND}(1-t)w - \left(1 - p^{FIND}\right)b - s \right]l + s = p^{FIND}(1-t)w.$$

One final step, moving the term s from the left-hand side to the right-hand side, gives the budget constraint in the requested form:

$$c + \left[p^{FIND}(1-t)w - \left(1 - p^{FIND}\right)b - s \right]l = \left[p^{FIND}(1-t)w - s \right].$$

b. As per the construction of any Lagrangian, the first component is the objective function to be optimized, and the second component is the constraint on the optimization (written appropriately and appended with the Lagrange multiplier):

$$u(c,l) + \lambda\left\{\left[p^{FIND}(1-t)w-s\right]-c-\left[p^{FIND}(1-t)w-\left(1-p^{FIND}\right)b-s\right]l\right\},$$

or, with the given utility function inserted,

$$\ln c - \frac{\theta}{1+1/\psi}\left(1-l\right)^{1+1/\psi} + \lambda\left\{\left[p^{FIND}(1-t)w-s\right]-c-\left[p^{FIND}(1-t)w-\left(1-p^{FIND}\right)b-s\right]l\right\}$$

(Either representation is fine, but the latter is more directly relevant for the subsequent analysis.)

c. The first-order conditions with respect to c and l, based on the Lagrangian above and the given utility function, are, respectively,

$$\frac{1}{c}-\lambda=0$$

and

$$\theta\left(1-l\right)^{1/\psi}-\lambda\left[p^{FIND}(1-t)w-\left(1-p^{FIND}\right)b-s\right]=0.$$

(As always, these first-order conditions are simply the respective partial derivatives of the Lagrangian with respect c and l, each set equal to zero. By this point, even though the analysis in this problem is more involved than in the examples studied in the chapter, setting up Lagrangians and computing first-order conditions should be conceptually clear.)

d. The FOC on c obtained above immediately tells us that $\lambda = 1/c$ at the optimal choice.

Inserting this expression for λ into the FOC on l obtained above gives

$$\theta\left(1-l\right)^{1/\psi} = \frac{1}{c}\left[p^{FIND}(1-t)w-\left(1-p^{FIND}\right)b-s\right].$$

Dividing both sides by $1/c$ gives

$$\frac{\theta\left(1-l\right)^{1/\psi}}{1/c} = p^{FIND}(1-t)w-\left(1-p^{FIND}\right)b-s$$

,

which is in the final requested form because the numerator on the left-hand side is the marginal utility of leisure, and the denominate on the left-hand side is the marginal utility of consumption. This expression is thus the consumption-leisure optimality condition for the search framework.

e. In the final expression obtained in part d, the right-hand side is the (absolute value of the) slope of the budget line—that is, the slope of the budget line is

$$-\left[p^{FIND}(1-t)w-\left(1-p^{FIND}\right)b-s\right],$$

which, notice, is a generalization of the slope of the budget constraint of the consumption-labor framework of chapter 2. In particular, if $p^{FIND} = 1$, $b = 0$, and $s = 0$, then the slope is -$(1-t)w$, just as in chapter 2.

In chapter 2, recall that the horizontal intercept of the budget line (i.e., the intercept on the leisure axis) was 1. Here the horizontal intercept is not 1. To determine what the horizontal intercept in this problem is, start from the budget constraint as expressed in, say, the final solution in part a. Suppose that $c = 0$ in the budget constraint; solving for l gives

$$\text{horizontal intercept} = \frac{\left[p^{FIND}(1-t)w-s \right]}{\left[p^{FIND}(1-t)w-s-\left(1-p^{FIND}\right)b \right]}.$$

Note the following observation: if $b = 0$ (i.e., temporarily substitute $b = 0$ into the above expression), then the horizontal intercept does simplify to 1 despite the presence of search frictions. But if $b > 0$, then the horizontal intercept does not equal 1.

If $b > 0$ and if $p^{FIND} < 1$, then it is clear that the term $(1 - p^{FIND})b > 0$. Hence, the term $\left[p^{FIND}(1-t)w-s \right] > \left[p^{FIND}(1-t)w-s-\left(1-p^{FIND}\right)b \right]$; that is, the numerator (excluding the multiple 1) of the previous expression is larger than the denominator of the previous expression. Hence, overall, the horizontal intercept is larger than 1. These observations are important for a full accounting in the subsequent analysis, though it makes the complete analysis cumbersome. Thus it was fine if you based the analysis only on the slope of the budget line and the induced changes in the optimal choice, and this is how the rest of the analysis proceeds.

Due to the economic downturn and associated sluggishness in employment, the government has been considering (and engaging in) various forms of interventions in labor markets aimed at increasing the welfare (the utility) of individuals. Based on the sketch in part e, you are to analyze various types of labor market interventions with a focus on determining whether or not they would increase the welfare (the utility) of the representative individual. (NOTE: You are not required to draw new sketches in the subsequent analysis, but you may do so if it clarifies your work.)

f. Based on the analysis in part e, a reduction in *t* increases the absolute value of the slope—that is, the budget line becomes steeper. However, the budget line does not simply pivot around the horizontal intercept in this case because, as the analysis in part e showed, the horizontal intercept is not fixed in this case.

However, focusing only on changes induced by the steepening of the budget line, as the conclusion in part e permitted, note that the new optimal choice (on the new steeper budget line) clearly has higher utility (because it lies on a higher indifference curve). The economic interpretation is that if individuals can take home a larger portion of their labor income as after-tax pay, they will be better off.

g. Based on the analysis in part e, an increase in *b* reduces the absolute value of the slope—that is, the budget line becomes flatter. However, the budget line does not pivot around the horizontal intercept in this case because, as the analysis in part e showed, the horizontal intercept is not fixed in this case.

So we want to use only the changes induced by the flattening of the budget line, as the conclusion in part e permitted, because the new optimal choice (on the new flatter budget line) clearly has lower utility (it lies on a lower indifference curve). The economic interpretation is that if individuals can receive a larger quantity of payments (unemployment benefits) by not working, it reduces their incentive to search for or accept jobs in the first place. This ultimately leads to lower utility, and to the extent that market (expected) wages are still higher than unemployment benefits.

h. Based on the analysis in part e, a reduction in *s* increases the absolute value of the slope—that is, the budget line becomes steeper. However, the budget line does not pivot around the horizontal intercept in this case because, as the analysis in part e showed, the horizontal intercept is not fixed in this case.

We need to use only the changes induced by the steepening of the budget line, as the conclusion in part e permitted, because the new optimal choice (on the new steeper budget line) clearly has higher utility (it lies on a higher indifference curve). The economic interpretation is that if it is less costly to search for a job, individuals will be willing to search harder for jobs, which means they are more likely to actually end up with a job, even if p^{FIND} is constant. This ultimately increases these individuals' welfare.

i. Based on the analysis in part e, an increase in p^{FIND} increases the absolute value of the slope—that is, the budget line becomes steeper. However, the budget line does not pivot around the horizontal intercept in this case because, as the analysis in part e showed, the horizontal intercept is not fixed in this case.

We need to use only the changes induced by the steepening of the budget line, as the conclusion in part e permitted, because the new optimal choice (on the new steeper budget line) clearly has higher utility (it lies on a higher indifference curve). The economic interpretation is that if it is more likely an individual will find a job, even holding constant how hard they look for a job, they will be better off.

Chapter 28 Problem Set Solutions

1. Matching-Market Clearing

All of the analysis below requires the "labor supply" function and the "labor demand" function, which are, respectively,

$$\theta = \left[\frac{h'(lfp)}{u'(c)} \cdot \frac{1}{w}\right]^{\frac{1}{1-\gamma}} \text{ and } \theta = \left[\frac{\omega}{A \cdot f'(n^D) - w}\right]^{-\frac{1}{\gamma}}.$$

a. The job-creation ("labor demand") expression shows that for any given n, an increase in A leads to an increase in θ. Hence the job-creation condition shifts outwards for any given θ. Each potential new hire is now marginally more productive, hence an increase in recruiting expenditures.

b. The LFP ("labor supply") expression, in and of itself, shows that A is not contained directly inside it. Thus there is no shift at all in LFP.

c. Together, the solutions in parts a and b suggest that equilibrium labor-market tightness θ^* increases and equilibrium labor n^* increases. The economics is that labor demand has shifted outward, holding constant the labor-supply function.

d. The job-creation ("labor demand") expression shows that for any given n, a decrease in A leads to a decrease in θ. Hence the job-creation condition shifts inwards for any given θ. Each potential new hire is now marginally less productive, hence a decrease in recruiting expenditures.

e. The LFP ("labor supply") expression, in and of itself, shows that A is not contained directly inside it. Thus there is no shift at all in LFP.

f. Together, the solutions in parts d and e suggest that equilibrium labor-market tightness θ^* decreases and equilibrium n^* decreases. The economics is that labor demand has shrunk, holding constant the labor-supply function.

g. The job-creation ("labor demand") expression shows that for any given n, an increase in ω leads to a decrease in θ. Hence the job-creation condition shifts inwards for any given θ. Each vacancy is now more expensive, hence a pullback in recruiting expenditures.

h. The LFP ("labor supply") expression, in and of itself, shows that ω is not contained directly inside it. Thus, there is no shift at all in LFP.

i. Together the solutions in parts h and I suggest that equilibrium labor-market tightness θ^* decreases and equilibrium n^* decreases. The economics is that labor demand has shrunk, holding constant the labor-supply function.

Chapter 29 Problem Set Solutions

1. Steady-State Analysis: LFP

a. Dropping the time subscripts and canceling the $u'(c)/u'(c)$ that then appear on the right-hand side gives us

$$\frac{h'(lfp)}{u'(c)} = p^{FIND} \cdot \left[(1-t) \cdot w + \beta(1-\rho) \cdot \left(\frac{h'(lfp)}{u'(c)} \right) \right] + (1-p^{FIND}) \cdot b .$$

Next, subtract from both sides

$$p^{FIND} \beta(1-\rho) \frac{h'(lfp)}{u'(c)} ,$$

which gives

$$\frac{h'(lfp)}{u'(c)} - p^{FIND} \beta(1-\rho) \left(\frac{h'(lfp)}{u'(c)} \right) = p^{FIND} \cdot (1-t) \cdot w + (1-p^{FIND}) \cdot b .$$

Collect the terms on the left-hand side so that

$$\frac{h'(lfp)}{u'(c)} \left(1 - p^{FIND} \beta(1-\rho) \right) = p^{FIND} \cdot (1-t) \cdot w + (1-p^{FIND}) \cdot b .$$

Finally, divide both sides by $\left(1 - p^{FIND} \beta(1-\rho) \right)$, which yields

$$\frac{h'(lfp)}{u'(c)} = \frac{p^{FIND} \cdot (1-t) \cdot w + (1-p^{FIND}) \cdot b}{1 - p^{FIND} \beta(1-\rho)} ,$$

which is in the final form requested.

b. The steady-state (aka, long-run) reservation wage is simply the right-hand side of the final expression from part a above.

3. Firms, Capital, and Labor-Market Turnover

a. The infinite sequence of employment constraints is the set of constraints on the profit maximization problem. The profit-maximization problem begins from the perspective of the start of period t, which means that profit terms and employment constraints beyond period t must be appropriately discounted. That is, everything about future periods must be appropriately discounted, just as in chapter 8, in which it was both utility and budget constraints beyond period t that were discounted.

Recall that in chapter 8, the appropriate discount factors, as we look successively down the timeline beyond period t, were β, β^2, β^3, β^4, …. In the firm optimization problem here, something similar is required. However, it is not successive powers of β that are needed (since the firm does not solve a utility maximization problem), but rather successive powers of $\frac{1}{1+r}$ that are needed. This follows from making an analogy between our two-period firm analysis in chapter 6 and our infinite-period consumer analysis in chapter 8: in our two-period firm analysis, recall that, in order to convert period-2 profits into present-discounted period-1 one terms, the "discount factor" (for the firm) $\frac{1}{1+r}$ was used. This was a one-period discounting—that is, discounting period-2 profits back one period to period 1. By analogy, discounting period-3 profits back two periods to period 1 would require the "discount factor" $\left(\dfrac{1}{1+r}\right)^{2} = \dfrac{1}{(1+r)^{2}}$; discounting period-4 profits back three periods to

period 1 would require the "discount factor" $\left(\dfrac{1}{1+r}\right)^{3} = \dfrac{1}{(1+r)^{3}}$, and so on.

Then, let the nondiscount-factor component of the multiplier on the period-t employment

constraint be λ_{t}, the nondiscount-factor component of the multiplier on the period-$t+1$

employment constraint be λ_{t+1} , the nondiscount-factor component of the multiplier on the

period-$t+2$ employment constraint be λ_{t+2} , and so on.

Putting all of the above logic together, we have the Lagrangian for the profit-

maximization problem

$$A_{t}f(k_{t},n_{t})+k_{t}-w_{t}n_{t}-k_{t+1}-\omega v_{t}+\left(\frac{1}{1+r}\right)\left[A_{t+1}f(k_{t+1},n_{t+1})+k_{t+1}-w_{t+1}n_{t+1}-k_{t+2}-\omega v_{t+1}\right]$$

$$+\left(\frac{1}{(1+r)^{2}}\right)\left[A_{t+2}f(k_{t+2},n_{t+2})+k_{t+2}-w_{t+2}n_{t+2}-k_{t+3}-\omega v_{t+2}\right]$$

$$+\left(\frac{1}{(1+r)^{3}}\right)\left[A_{t+3}f(k_{t+3},n_{t+3})+k_{t+3}-w_{t+3}n_{t+3}-k_{t+4}-\omega v_{t+3}\right]+...(\text{infinite number of terms})$$

$$+\lambda_{t}\left[(1-\rho)n_{t}+v_{t}q_{t}^{FIND}-n_{t+1}\right]+\left(\frac{\lambda_{t+1}}{1+r}\right)\left[(1-\rho)n_{t+1}+v_{t+1}q_{t+1}^{FIND}-n_{t+2}\right]$$

$$+\left(\frac{\lambda_{t+2}}{(1+r)^{2}}\right)\left[(1-\rho)n_{t+2}+v_{t+2}q_{t+2}^{FIND}-n_{t+3}\right]$$

$$+\left(\frac{\lambda_{t+3}}{(1+r)^{3}}\right)\left[(1-\rho)n_{t+3}+v_{t+3}q_{t+3}^{FIND}-n_{t+4}\right]+...(\text{infinite number of terms})$$

b. Given the effort of constructing the Lagrangian, the first-order conditions are easy to compute.

The FOC with respect to k_{t+1} is

$$-1+\left(\frac{1}{1+r}\right)\left[A_{t+1}f_{k}(k_{t+1},n_{t+1})+1\right]=0 .$$

c. The FOC in part b is identical to the FOC on capital accumulation from our analysis of the baseline two-period firm profit-maximization problem. Thus search aspects of labor markets do not at all alter the capital demand function (recall that the FOC in part b **is** the capital demand function, when solved for r).

d. Simply reading the Lagrangian in part a, the FOC with respect to v_t is

$$-\omega + \lambda_t q_t^{FIND} = 0;$$

the FOC with respect to n_{t+1} is

$$-\left(\frac{1}{1+r}\right)\left(A_{t+1}f_n(k_{t+1},n_{t+1}) - w_{t+1}\right) - \lambda_t + \left(\frac{\lambda_{t+1}}{1+r}\right)(1-\rho) = 0;$$

and the FOC with respect to v_{t+1} is

$$-\left(\frac{1}{1+r}\right)\omega + \left(\frac{\lambda_{t+1}}{1+r}\right)q_{t+1}^{FIND} = 0 \quad.$$

e. The first FOC in part d can be solved for the multiplier: $\lambda_t = \dfrac{\omega}{q_t^{FIND}}$. Similarly the third FOC in part d can be solved for the multiplier: $\lambda_{t+1} = \dfrac{\omega}{q_{t+1}^{FIND}}$. (Note the recursive property that emerges here, which, as we saw in chapters 3, 4, and 8, is a property that emerges from any sequential Lagrangian analysis.)

Substituting these expressions for λ_t and λ_{t+1} into the second FOC in part d gives

$$\left(\frac{1}{1+r}\right)\left(A_{t+1}f_n(k_{t+1},n_{t+1}) - w_{t+1}\right) - \frac{\omega}{q_t^{FIND}} + \left(\frac{\omega/q_{t+1}^{FIND}}{1+r}\right)(1-\rho) = 0.$$

Getting to the final requested expression requires one further rearrangement. Isolate the term $\dfrac{\omega}{q_t^{FIND}}$ so that

$$\frac{\omega}{q_t^{FIND}} = \left(\frac{1}{1+r}\right)\left(A_{t+1}f_n(k_{t+1},n_{t+1}) - w_{t+1}\right) + \left(\frac{\omega / q_{t+1}^{FIND}}{1+r}\right)(1-\rho).$$

It is fine if you stopped here, since this does satisfy the requested form. However, let's go one step further, and factor the term $\dfrac{1}{1+r}$ (which is just the discount factor) out of the right-hand side, and this gives

$$\frac{\omega}{q_t^{FIND}} = \left(\frac{1}{1+r}\right)\left(A_{t+1}f_n(k_{t+1},n_{t+1}) - w_{t+1} + (1-\rho)\frac{\omega}{q_{t+1}^{TURNOVER}}\right).$$

The expression you obtained in part e is the job creation condition. In the remainder of the analysis, you will compare and contrast the job creation condition with the "labor demand" condition studied in chapter 6. For the remainder of the analysis, you may (but do not need to) suppose that the production function is Cobb-Douglas: $f(k_t,n_t) = k_t^\alpha n_t^{1-\alpha}$, with $\alpha \in (0,1)$.

f. Imposing $\rho = 1$ on the job creation condition obtained in part e, we have

$$\frac{\omega}{q_t^{FIND}} = \left(\frac{1}{1+r}\right)\left(A_{t+1}f_n(k_{t+1},n_{t+1}) - w_{t+1}\right).$$

To interpret this condition (or even the full job creation condition in part e), think in terms of basic "marginal benefit equals marginal cost" terms. This basic principle is the basis for economic interpretation/intuition of the result of any economic optimization analysis (not just with respect to firm theory or even just macroeconomic analysis).

The right-hand side of the condition immediately above is the present discounted value of the marginal benefit to a firm of successfully recruiting a worker in period t. Recalling the timing of events described above, a worker that is successfully recruited in period t only begins working at the firm in period $t+1$ (and in the special case being analyzed here, only works for the firm in period $t+1$, because there is a probability equal to one (i.e., a 100 percent chance) that the individual will not be working for the firm in period $t+2$). In period $t+1$, the marginal output that the new recruit brings to the firm is $A_{t+1} f_n(k_{t+1}, n_{t+1})$ (i.e., the marginal product of labor in period $t+1$), and the wage the firm must pay the worker is w_{t+1}. Thus (using terminology that should be familiar from microeconomics) the marginal revenue product of the worker in period $t+1$ is $A_{t+1} f_n(k_{t+1}, n_{t+1}) - w_{t+1}$. But because the recruiting decisions of the firm are made in period t, this marginal revenue product is discounted by $1+r$.

The left-hand side of the condition reflects the marginal cost of recruiting. There is the direct cost ω of recruiting; this cost is adjusted for the fact that recruiting only has a probability of success q_t^{FIND}.

Thus the condition has the interpretation that the marginal cost of successful recruiting equals the (present-value) marginal benefit of successful recruiting.

g. Imposing $\rho = 1$ and $q_t^{FIND} = q_{t+1}^{FIND} = 1$ on the job creation condition obtained in part e, we have

$$\omega = \left(\frac{1}{1+r}\right)\left(A_{t+1} f_n(k_{t+1}, n_{t+1}) - w_{t+1}\right).$$

The interpretation is identical to that in part f, except now when a firm begins the recruiting process by spending ω, it knows that it will hire an employee for sure (because the probability of finding a worker is $q_t^{FIND} = 1$).

h. The labor demand condition that emerged from the firm analysis in chapter 6 was that the marginal product of labor equals the real wage in every period. In terms of the notation of this problem, that means $A_t f_n(k_t, n_t) = w_t$, $A_{t+1} f_n(k_{t+1}, n_{t+1}) = w_{t+1}$, $A_{t+2} f_n(k_{t+2}, n_{t+2}) = w_{t+2}$, ...

On inspecting the job creation condition in part e, as well as their successive simplifications in parts f and g, it should be clear that the only way the simple labor demand condition can emerge is if all three of the following conditions are satisfied: $\rho = 1$ and

$$q_t^{FIND} = q_{t+1}^{FIND} = q_{t+2}^{FIND} = q_{t+3}^{FIND} = ...1, \text{ and } \omega = 0.$$

To see this more explicitly, simply impose on the job creation condition of part e that $\rho = 1$, $q_t^{FIND} = 1$, and $\omega = 0$. We are then left simply with $A_{t+1} f_n(k_{t+1}, n_{t+1}) = w_{t+1}$, which is the labor demand condition we studied earlier.

A much more general point emerges from this analysis: the standard (i.e., basic microeconomics) notion of demand (here, labor demand, but the more general point has nothing to do with labor markets per se) is a special case of the predictions of search theory. The standard notion of demand can be thought of as search activity in the special case that if one searches, one will find what one is looking for with certainty (in this case, searching for workers, but the point could be more general—say, searching for consumer goods); that if one finds what one is looking for, one will only use/need it for one period (rather than multiple time periods); and that it is costless to search.

Thus search theory really is a generalization of the basic theory of supply and demand— generalization meaning that it allows one to consider all of the same issues (whether microeconomic or macroeconomic) for which supply/demand analysis is useful, but it also allows for considering richer issues (e.g., How long do workers stay at a job? How likely is it a suitable match will be found?). This generalization of the basic theory of supply and demand, which is the staple of all economic analysis, is part of the reason that Diamond, Mortensen, and Pissarides were awarded the Nobel Prize in 2010.

Chapter 30 Problem Set Questions

1. Optimal SOE Choices with and without Foreign Credit Constraints: A Numerical Analysis

Suppose that in the period-1 consumption aggregator

$$\omega(c_{1,H}, c_{1,ROW}) = \left[\sigma \cdot c_{1,H}^{\rho} + (1-\sigma) \cdot c_{1,ROW}^{\rho}\right]^{1/\rho}$$ that $\sigma = 0$, which implies that $c_1 = c_{1,ROW}$. Similarly,

for the period-2 consumption aggregator, $\omega(c_{2,H}, c_{2,ROW}) = \left[\sigma \cdot c_{2,H}^{\rho} + (1-\sigma) \cdot c_{2,ROW}^{\rho}\right]^{1/\rho}$, if $\sigma = 0$,

then $c_2 = c_{2,ROW}$.

Lifetime preferences of the representative SOE consumer are described by the utility

function

$$u(c_1, c_2) = \sqrt{c_1} + \beta \sqrt{c_2},$$

where c_1 denotes consumption in period 1 and c_2 denotes consumption in period 2. The

parameter β is known is the subjective discount factor and measures the SOE consumer's degree

of impatience: the smaller is β, the higher the weight the SOE consumer assigns to present

consumption compared to future consumption.

Suppose that $\beta = 1/1.1$. The representative SOE household has initial real net foreign

wealth of $(1 + r_{ROW})a_{0,ROW} = 1$, and has endowment $y_1 = 5$ units of goods in period 1 and

endowment $y_2 = 10$ units of goods in period 2. The real interest rate paid on foreign assets held

from period 1 to period 2 is $r_{ROW} = 0.1$, and the real exchange rate $e_1 = 1$ and $e_2 = 1$.

a. For the given utility function, calculate the equilibrium levels of consumption in periods 1

and 2. (Hint: Set up the Lagrangian and solve.)

Solution   The SOE consumer's problem is to maximize lifetime utility—given by $u(c_1, c_2)$—subject to the SOE LBC. The Lagrangian for this problem is

$$L(c_1, c_2, \lambda) = u(c_1, c_2) + \lambda \left((1 + r_{ROW}) a_{0,ROW} + y_1 + \frac{y_2}{1 + r_{ROW}} - c_1 - \frac{c_2}{1 + r_{ROW}} \right),$$

in which the nonzero initial real net foreign wealth $(1 + r_{ROW}) a_{0,ROW}$ is included. The first-order conditions with respect to c_1 and c_2 are

$$u_1(c_1, c_2) - \lambda = 0$$
$$u_2(c_1, c_2) - \frac{\lambda}{1 + r_1} = 0$$

Combining these, we get the SOE's consumption-savings optimality condition, $u_1(c_1, c_2) = (1 + r_{ROW}) u_2(c_1, c_2)$ (i.e., the MRS equals the slope of the LBC). Using the given utility function, at the optimal choice the following condition must be satisfied:

$$\frac{1}{2\sqrt{c_1}} = (1 + r_1) \frac{\beta}{2\sqrt{c_2}}.$$

Solving this expression for c_2 as a function of c_1 gives $c_2 = (1 + r_{ROW})^2 \beta^2 c_1$. With the specific numerical values given, this turns out to be $c_2 = c_1$. Substituting this into the lifetime budget constraint yields

$$c_1 + \frac{c_1}{1 + r_{ROW}} = (1 + r_{ROW}) a_{0,ROW} + y_1 + \frac{y_2}{1 + r_{ROW}}.$$

Solving for c_1 gives

$$c_1 = \left[\frac{1 + r_{ROW}}{2 + r_{ROW}} \right] \left[(1 + r_{ROW})a_{0,ROW} + y_1 + \frac{y_2}{1 + r_{ROW}} \right],$$

which, when using the numerical values provided, yields $c_1 = 7.90$ and hence $c_2 = 7.90$.

Note also that although you were not asked to compute it, you could find the implied value for $a_{1,ROW}$ using the period-1 budget constraint $c_1 + a_{1,ROW} = (1 + r_{ROW})a_{0,ROW} + y_1$. This yields that $a_{1,ROW} = -1.9$, indicating that the SOE economy chooses to be a debtor at the end of period 1.

a. Starting from your solutions in part a, calculate the SOE's trade balance in period 1 (tb_1) and current account in period 1.

Solution Using the definition of the trade balance, we have $tb_1 = y_1 - e_1 \cdot c_{1,ROW}$. Next, note that due to the preference specification presented, $c_1 = c_{1,ROW}$ — meaning all of the SOE's (optimal) consumption purchases are imported goods. Then, using the numerical values provided for y_1 and e_1, we find the SOE's trade balance to be $tb_1 = 5 - 7.90 = -2.90$.

So the current account in period 1, per its definition, is $tb_1 + r_{ROW}a_{0,ROW} = -2.81$.

c. Suppose now that foreign lenders to this SOE economy impose credit constraints on domestic SOE consumers. Specifically, foreign lenders impose the tightest possible credit constraint—SOE consumers are not allowed to be in debt at the end of period 1, which implies that the SOE consumer's real wealth at the end of period 1 must be nonnegative ($a_{1,ROW} \geq 0$). What is the SOE's optimal choices of period-1 and period-2 consumption under this cross-country credit restriction? Briefly explain, either logically or graphically or both.

Solution The imposition of these credit constraints will be binding on the SOE consumer's behavior. That is, it will alter the choices made by the SOE, as can be seen from the fact that in the absence of the credit constraints in part a, the SOE chose to be in debt at the end of period 1.

The SOE, if restricted to hold a nonnegative foreign asset position at the end of period 1, will choose that asset position closest to its unrestricted choice, but one that also satisfies the ROW's credit constraint—that is, the SOE will end up period 1 with $a_{1,ROW} = 0$.

The period-1 budget constraint, $c_1 + a_{1,ROW} = (1 + r_{ROW})a_{0,ROW} + y_1$ then implies that $c_1 = 6$. The SOE will simply consume all it can in period 1, which is the sum of its endowment and initial foreign assets.

It remains now to solve numerically for c_2. Based on the period-2 budget constraint, $c_2 + a_{2,ROW} = (1 + r_{ROW})a_{1,ROW} + y_2$ (plus the condition $a_2 = 0$ imposed and $a_{1,ROW} = 0$), it must be that $c_2 = y_2 = 10$.

d.   Does the credit constraint described in part b enhance or diminish the welfare of the SOE economy (i.e., does it increase or decrease lifetime utility)?

Solution With the values for consumption in each of the two periods from parts a and c, the utility function shows that utility without foreign credit constraints equals $u(c_1, c_2) = 5.34$ and utility with credit constraints is $u(c_1, c_2) = 5.29$. The SOE's welfare is thus lower under imposition of credit sanctions.

SOE Government Sovereignty and the Consequences of Sanctions

Consider a two-period model of the SOE government, with g_1 and g_2 denoting real government spending in periods 1 and 2, and t_1 and t_2 denoting real lump-sum taxes collected by the government in periods 1 and 2.

The consideration of the government's "utility" function likely involves more than simple economic considerations. Nonetheless, one can study what a government (whether SOE or not) would choose to do if it had some particular some utility function.

Suppose that the SOE government's lifetime utility function is

$$g_1 - t_1$$

That is, the government only cares (in terms of utils) about period-1 government spending net of tax collections. However, due to political considerations, there is an upper limit of 100 on how large a fiscal surplus can be run in period 2.

The government's lifetime budget constraint is

$$g_1 + \frac{g_2}{1+r} = t_1 + \frac{t_2}{1+r} + (1+r)b_0,$$

with r denoting the real interest rate. For simplicity, suppose throughout this problem that $r = 0$. The government's real asset position at the start of period 1 is b_0, at the end of period 1 is b_1, and (as usual in the two-period analysis of the government) at the end of period 2 is $b_2 = 0$.

Suppose that the SOE government begins period 1 with a negative asset position—that is, suppose $b_0 < 0$.

If $b_0 < 0$, is the government in debt at the beginning of period 1? Or is it impossible to determine? Justify/explain in no more than two phrases/sentences.

Solution By definition, b_{t-1} is the government's net asset position at the start of any period t. Thus a negative value means a net debt position; the government is thus in debt at the beginning of period 1.

Suppose the government can possibly choose to reset b_0 to zero. That is, by sovereign right of being a government, suppose it can simply "announce" that $b_0 = 0$ even though, absent any such announcement, $b_0 < 0$. Would resetting b_0 to zero possibly allow the government to reach higher lifetime utility? Or would it necessarily decrease the lifetime utility the government could reach? Or would it leave the lifetime utility the government could reach unchanged? Or is it impossible to determine? Briefly, but thoroughly, justify/explain.

Solution To address this question (as well as part c), it is helpful to rewrite the lifetime budget constraint given above as

$$g_1 - t_1 = \frac{t_2 - g_2}{1+r} + (1+r)b_0.$$

What is useful about this rewriting of the budget constraint is that the term $g_1 - t_1$ (which is the government's lifetime utility function) appears on the left-hand side. You are given that $r = 0$ and that $t_2 - g_2$ (i.e., the fiscal surplus in period two) cannot be larger than 100. With a strictly negative b_0, the right-hand side is necessarily strictly smaller than 100, which in turn implies that $g_1 - t_1$ is necessarily strictly smaller than 100. If the government can reset b_0 to zero, then the right-hand side could be as large as 100, which in turn implies that $g_1 - t_1$ could be as large as

100. Thus this policy choice (which is a government "default" on its existing debt obligations) allows the government to achieve higher lifetime utility.

a. Suppose that the government can not only possibly choose to reset b_0 to zero (as in part b above), but it could also choose to reset b_0 to a strictly positive value (i.e., it could choose to set some $b_0 > 0$). However, if it does set b_0 to a strictly positive value, the rest of the world imposes "sanctions" on this country's government, which the government is fully aware of. These sanctions cause two things to happen:

   i.   Any positive b_0 that the government decides it has are removed by the sanctions; that is, the sanctions cause b_0 to fall back to exactly zero.

   ii. The world's financial markets prohibit this particular government from borrowing at all during period 1.

Taking into account the consequences of the sanctions, would resetting b_0 to a strictly positive value possibly allow the government to reach higher lifetime utility? Or would it necessarily decrease the lifetime utility the government could reach? Or would it leave the lifetime utility the government could reach unchanged? Or is it impossible to determine? In answering this question, the policy choice of comparison should be the utility consequences of resetting b_0 to zero that was analyzed in part b. Briefly, but thoroughly, justify/explain.

   If the goal of the government is to maximize its lifetime utility, answer two related questions:

   i.   What should it choose to do regarding b0? That is, should it leave the b0 < 0 as is, should it choose to reset b0 to zero (as in part b), or should it choose to reset b0 to a strictly positive value (as in part c)?

   ii. What value for $g_1 - t_1$ should it set in period 1?

(NOTE: You are to answer both of these questions, and keep in mind the setup of the question described above.) Briefly, but thoroughly, justify/explain.

Solution The analysis in part b concluded that if the government "chose" to move to a higher level of b_0 (i.e., moving from strictly negative b_0 to $b_0 = 0$), it would be able to achieve higher lifetime utility. It may stand to reason then that moving to a strictly positive b_0 would enable it to achieve an even higher utility.

With the sanctions described, however, this is impossible. If the SOE government attempts to set $b_0 > 0$ (which is tantamount to the government "creating assets" for itself), the sanctions lower b_0 down to zero (which can be interpreted as governments in the rest of the world "seizing" the government's newly created "assets"). Moreover, and important, the SOE government cannot spend more in period one than its tax collections in period 1 as a consequence of the second component of the sanctions.

The latter conclusion follows from inspecting the budget constraint as expressed in part b along with the following argument: with $b_0 = 0$ (due to the first component of the sanctions) and the impossibility of setting $t_2 - g_2$ larger than 100, the government could run a fiscal deficit in period 1 of $g_1 - t_1$ of as large as 100. But, in order to do so, the government would have to borrow in period 1 (i.e., be in debt at the end of period 1).

The second component of the sanctions prevents the SOE government from borrowing in period 1; hence the best the government can do is implement $g_1 - t_1 = 0$ in period 1.

Thus choosing to "create assets" necessarily decreases the lifetime utility the SOE government could achieve, given the nature of sanctions that would be imposed on the country.

Chapter 31 Problem Set Solutions

1. **The Hazards of Fixed Exchange Rates**

a. Use the interest parity condition. If the peg is expected to remain in place, that means $E_{t+1}^e = E_t$, so the interest parity condition tells us that the domestic nominal interest rate equals the foreign real interest, so $i_t = r^* = 0.10$ during this time.

b. Because, as we just found in part a, the domestic nominal interest rate is constant during this period, money demand (and hence in equilibrium money supply) must also be constant during this period. If money supply is unchanging, seignorage revenue must be zero.

c. Recall the government budget constraint is $B_t^G - B_{t-1}^G = \dfrac{M_t - M_{t-1}}{E_t} - DEF_t$. Seignorage revenue is zero during this period, so the government budget constraint reduces to $B_t^G - B_{t-1}^G = -DEF_t$. The left-hand side is the change in foreign reserves during period t, which is our definition of the balance of payments. That is, a country's BOP during a particular period equals the change in its foreign reserves during that period. With $DEF = 5.5$, clearly the BOP deficit is 5.5 in every period.

d. With a completely unanticipated devaluation, the nominal interest rate will never rise therefore seignorage revenue will never become negative (i.e., there will never be a currency run), so the only drain on foreign reserves is the fiscal deficit. With a fiscal deficit of 5.5 and the government currently holding foreign reserves of 22, clearly it will take 4 periods for the government to run out of foreign reserves at which point the fixed exchange rate will have to be abandoned.

e. Again use the interest parity condition. Now we have $E_{t+1}^e = (1+\mu)E_t = 1.5E_t$, so the interest parity condition becomes $1 + i = (1.1) \cdot 1.5$, and the domestic nominal interest rate in the current period is $i = 0.65$. The domestic nominal interest rate rises when the devaluation is imminent because in order to be induced to hold an asset denominated in a currency that is about to weaken investors have to be compensated with a higher return.

f. In the period before the exchange rate collapses, the nominal interest rate rises to 65 percent (computed in part e). Money demand in this period (plug into the given money demand function) is thus $\phi = 11 - 10 \cdot 0.65 = 4.5$. Next compute money demand one period earlier: because the nominal interest rate was 10 percent one period earlier, money demand was $\phi = 11 - 10 \cdot 0.10 = 10$. Thus money demand (and hence the money supply) falls by 5.5. The reason is a run on the currency—holders of the peso want to get out of pesos before the collapse of the exchange rate, and the money supply shrinks as citizens turn their pesos over to the central bank in exchange for dollars. Thus in this period (the balance of payments crisis) foreign reserves fall by $5.5 + 5.5 = 11$ (5.5 due to the fiscal deficit plus 5.5 due to the negative seignorage revenue). Thus the peg only lasts three periods now—at the end of period 1, foreign reserves are $22 - 5.5 = 16.5$, at the end of period 2, foreign reserves are $16.5 - 5.5 = 11$, and at the end of period 3, foreign reserves are $11 - 11 = 0$.

3. BOP Crises

The two conditions needed to address questions a through d are the interest parity condition

$$(1+i) = (1+r^*)\frac{E^e_{t+1}}{E_t}$$

and the government budget constraint expressed in the form

$$B_t^G - B_{t-1}^G = \frac{M_t - M_{t-1}}{E_t} - DEF_t .$$

In the latter expression, use has been made of the fact that $P_t = E_t$, which follows from the assumptions of PPP and a constant foreign price level; in the former expression, the constant foreign price level (i.e., foreign inflation equals zero) allows us to use the real world interest rate rather than the nominal world interest rate.

a. A fixed exchange rate implies that the rate of devaluation is zero—which is simply another way of saying that $E_{t+1}^e = E_t = E$ always. The interest parity condition then shows that the domestic nominal interest rate equals the world real interest rate, 10 percent. Also recall that under a fixed exchange rate, which is expected to remain in place, seignorage revenue is zero—that is, $M_t = M_{t-1}$ as long as the peg is expected to remain in place.

b. With the peg in place, the government budget constraint reduces to $B_t^G - B_{t-1}^G = -DEF_t$. With the government currently holding net foreign reserves of 10 and running a deficit of 1 every period, the longest that the peg can remain in place with an unchanged fiscal budget is 10 periods. That is, the fiscal deficit draws foreign reserves down by one unit every period until $B^G = 0$. At that point, either the fiscal deficits have to come to an end or the peg has to be abandoned (or both).

Suppose that foreign reserves have now fallen to $B^G = 2$ (i.e., at the very beginning of the current period foreign reserve holdings are 2), and that the fiscal deficit remains as above. Suppose further that domestic residents now anticipate a devaluation of the domestic currency in the next period, and that the expected rate of depreciation between the current period and the next period is 10 percent. Call this expected rate of depreciation μ, so that $\mu = 0.10$.

c. With citizens expecting a 10 percent devaluation in the next period, we have that E_{t+1}^e is 10 percent higher than E_t—that is, $E_{t+1}^e = 1.1E_t$. From the interest parity condition, we then have that in the current period,

Thus, the nominal interest rate in the current period is $i_t = 0.21$, which is higher than the world interest rate of $r* = 0.10$. The economic intuition for why the nominal interest rate rises when a devaluation is expected is because in order to be willing to hold assets that are denominated in terms of a currency that will be getting weaker investors have to receive a higher return—that is, the interest rate on an asset denominated in a currency about to depreciate has to be higher than if that currency is not about to depreciate in order for people to still be willing to hold it.

d. In the current period the exchange rate has not yet collapsed, but it is expected to in the next period. As we just found in part c, this means the nominal interest rate rises—in particular, the nominal interest rate this period is higher than it was last period. This in turn means that money demand this period is smaller than money demand was last period because the money demand function decreases as the nominal interest rate rises. So people want to hold less of the domestic currency because they expect it will depreciate very soon. In money market equilibrium, this means money supply also falls—that is, the money supply this period is smaller than it was last period. This is what it means for seignorage revenue to be negative in the current period.

e. Proceed as we outlined in the chapter. Let's say that period T is the period in which the exchange rate finally collapses—it is thus a numerical value for T that we seek. As discussed in the chapter, it is period $T-1$ in which the BOP crisis occurs, meaning it is in period $T-1$ that people expect an imminent devaluation. The expectation of an imminent devaluation causes a rise in the nominal interest rate in period $T-1$ to $i_{T-1} = 0.21$, exactly as we found in part c above. For every period 0, 1, 2, …, $T-2$, though, because no devaluation was imminent, the nominal interest rate was $i = 0.10$.

We know that when the current period nominal interest rate is unchanged from the previous period's nominal interest rate that current-period seignorage revenue is zero (simply because money demand is the same in each of those periods). So for the first $T-2$ periods, the only drain on foreign reserves is the fiscal deficit. That is, for each of the first $T-2$ periods of the peg, foreign reserves fall by one each period.

In period $T-1$, however, because the nominal interest rate rises, we saw in part d that seignorage revenue is negative. In period $T-1$, nominal money demand is given by $M_{T-1} = E_{T-1}\phi(i_{T-1})$, but since $E_{T-1} = 1$ (i.e., the fixed exchange rate, which has not yet collapsed, is 1), we have that $M_{T-1} = \phi(i_{T-1})$. By similar logic, we have that in period $T-2$, $M_{T-2} = \phi(i_{T-2})$. Seignorage revenue in period $T-1$ is thus

$$\frac{\phi(i_{T-1}) - \phi(i_{T-2})}{E_{T-1}} = \frac{100 - 9.0909 i_{T-1} - (100 - 9.0909 i_{T-2})}{1}$$
$$= 9.0909(i_{T-2} - i_{T-1})$$
$$= 9.0909(0.10 - 0.21)$$
$$= -1$$

The negative seignorage revenue pulls foreign reserves down in period $T-1$ in addition to the fiscal deficit. That is, in period $T-1$,

$$B_T^G - B_{T-1}^G = \frac{M_{T-1} - M_{T-2}}{E_{T-1}} - DEF_{T-1}$$

and the first term on the right-hand side is not zero in period $T-1$. So in period $T-1$, foreign reserves fall by two units, whereas for the first $T-2$ periods they fell by one unit each period due to the deficit.

With all of this, we can conclude that it takes nine periods for the exchange rate to collapse, rather than the ten periods we found in part b when people never anticipated the devaluation. The reason the exchange rate collapse occurs faster when people anticipate a collapse is a currency run—shortly before the collapse, people want to get rid of the domestic currency because it is going to be worthless very soon and they would rather hold the foreign currency. The central bank (in reality, through the banking system, but here we're pretending that people deal directly with the central bank), must honor its fixed exchange rate which is still in place, so it loses foreign reserves even more quickly (the negative seignorage revenue) when the devaluation is imminent. This speeds up the process (kind of a self-fulfilling prophecy): the exchange rate collapses (sooner) because people expect it to collapse.